The Encyclopedia of the
Winter Olympics

The Encyclopedia of the
Winter Olympics

Written by John Wukovits

FRANKLIN WATTS
A Division of Scholastic Inc.

New York • Toronto • London • Auckland • Sydney
Mexico City • New Delhi • Hong Kong
Danbury, Connecticut

Developed for Franklin Watts by Visual Education Corporation, Princeton, New Jersey

Project Director: Jewel G. Moulthrop
Editor: Joseph Ziegler
Copyediting: Helen Castro, Eleanor Hero
Photo Research: Susan Buschhorn
Production Supervisor: Sara Matthews
Cover Design: Maxson Crandall
Interior Design: John Romer
Electronic Preparation: Fiona Torphy
Electronic Production: Rob Ehlers, Lisa Evans-Skopas

The use of Olympic-related marks and terminology is authorized by the U.S. Olympic Committee pursuant to the Ted Stevens Olympic and Amateur Sports Act (36 U.S.C. § 220506).

The editorial materials presented in this publication are the sole responsibility of Franklin Watts, a Division of Scholastic Inc.

Library of Congress Cataloging-in-Publication Data
Wukovits, John F., 1944-
     The encyclopedia of the Winter Olympics / written by John Wukovits.
        p.   cm. — (Watts reference)
     Includes bibliographical references and index.
     ISBN 0-531-11885-1 (lib. bdg.)   0-531-15452-1 (pbk.)
        1. Winter Olympics—Encyclopedias—Juvenile literature. [1. Winter
Olympics—Encyclopedias.] I. Title. II. Series.
GV841.5 .W85   2001
796.98'03 — dc21   2001027734

Printed in the United States

1 2 3 4 5 6 7 8 9 10 R 10 09 08 07 06 05 04 03 02 01

TABLE OF CONTENTS

Note: In this book you will find separate articles about the athletes whose names appear in SMALL CAPITAL LETTERS. Check the Table of Contents for the appropriate page numbers.

OLYMPIC HISTORY

According to legend, the Olympic Games commemorated the victory of Zeus, the most important Greek god, who had defeated his father, Kronos, for control of the world. The most widely accepted story about the origins of the games tells of a young man named Pelops who outwitted King Oenomaus of Pisatis, Greece. Oenomaus had offered the hand of his beautiful daughter, Hippodameia, in marriage to any man who could take her away from her home by chariot and successfully evade the king's pursuit. Thirteen men accepted the challenge, but each one was overtaken by the king—who owned the fastest horses in the land—and put to death.

In what can be judged as the first of many Olympic controversies, Pelops rigged the contest so that he would win. He offered half of the kingdom to the king's charioteer, Myrtilos, if he would damage a wheel axle so that it would break while the king chased after him. Myrtilos agreed. The chariot wheel broke as planned, and the king was thrown from the chariot and died from a broken neck.

Participants in the ancient Olympic Games entered the stadium from a sacred grove in which the temple of Zeus was located.

To memorialize his victory, Pelops established the Olympic Games in a valley called Olympia in western Greece, where the king died. The date of the first Olympic Games, 776 B.C., was so heralded in ancient Greece that it was considered the founding date of that nation. There was only one event, a footrace of approximately 630 feet, which was won by a sprinter named Coroebus.

Thereafter, athletes gathered every four years at Olympia to compete in a variety of events. At first the games were attended only by men from the regions around Olympia, but gradually renowned athletes from other parts of Greece and the Mediterranean joined.

All athletes competed naked in the stadium that had been built at Olympia. The dirt track, which measured about 215 yards long and 35 yards wide, was surrounded on all sides by grassy slopes where 40,000 spectators could sit. Nothing interfered with the games—wars were halted, and all trade among cities stopped. For the duration of the games, no man bearing weapons was permitted near Olympia. The games were considered so sacred that even in 480 B.C., when a few hundred men from the Greek city-state of Sparta fought to the death at Thermopylae against the mighty Persian army to save the nation, thousands of Greeks ignored the threat to their safety and attended the games.

The International Olympic Committee (IOC) approves the events that are included in the Olympics and selects the host cities. Members of the first IOC, including the founder of the modern Olympic Games, Baron Pierre de Coubertin (second from left), are shown here.

The games continued until A.D. 393, when Roman emperor Theodosius I, a Christian, banned the games as a pagan activity and ordered the huge statues of Greek gods at Olympia dismantled. During the following centuries, earthquakes and floods buried the stadium at Olympia, which became a distant memory of a once-proud Greek empire.

The Olympic Revival

The Olympic Games disappeared for the next 15 centuries. Stories of glorious triumphs and epic achievements at Olympia sometimes circulated, but no movement arose to renew the games until a Frenchman, Baron Pierre de Coubertin, revived the idea in the late 1800s. Born in Paris in 1863, Coubertin had a lifelong passion for sports. When he heard that a team of German archaeologists was uncovering the ruins at Olympia, Coubertin visited the Greek site and became fascinated with ancient Greek customs. He decided that a revival of the Olympic Games would restore pride in amateur sports and promote world peace.

At a meeting of the Athletic Sports Union in Paris in 1892, Coubertin proposed a gathering of athletes in all sports for the purpose of fellowship, athletics, and world peace: "Let us export oarsmen, runners, fencers . . . and on that day when it shall take place among the customs of Europe, the cause of peace will have received a new and powerful support."

Although his idea was greeted less than enthusiastically, Coubertin persisted, talking to athletic organizations around the world. In 1894 he met with delegates from nine nations, including Russia and the United States, to discuss amateur athletics. At this meeting he announced his plan to revive the Olympic Games. He spoke so passionately that he won the support of the delegates. Coubertin hoped to have the games coincide with the Paris International Exposition of 1900 and the start of the 20th century, but the delegates had other ideas.

The members voted unanimously to organize the first modern games in 1896. Appropriately, they selected Athens, Greece, as the site for the games. Coubertin chose the words *cittius, altius, fortius* to serve as the Olympic motto. The words are Latin for "faster, higher, stronger." They describe what athletes in the Olympics strive for: to be the best.

The Olympic Spirit Returns

Thirteen nations, including Greece, the United States, and Great Britain, sent 311 athletes to the 1896 Olympics. On April 6, about 80,000 spectators gathered to watch athletes compete in track and field events, swimming, wrestling, weightlifting, cycling, fencing, gymnastics, shooting, and lawn tennis. James B. Connolly of the United States became the first champion of the modern Olympics when he won the triple jump, receiving for his effort a diploma, a crown of olive branches, and a silver medal (gold was then considered too elaborate).

The inhabitants of Greece erupted in delight when their countryman Spyridon Louis sped to victory in the marathon, an event established to honor an epic moment in Greek history. As

WOMEN NOT ALLOWED

During the ancient Greek Olympics, women were not permitted either to participate in the activities or even to watch them. The competition was strictly for men, who performed in the nude. Any woman caught at the games was sentenced to death, taken to a nearby cliff, and thrown over.

Louis entered the rebuilt Olympic stadium, Greek princes George and Constantine joined him on the track.

Coubertin saw his idea realized. He further embellished his legacy when he created the Olympic flag and presented it to the Congress of Paris in 1914. The Olympic symbol appeared on a plain white background in the center of the flag. The five interlocking rings that make up the Olympic logo represent the major continents: Africa, the Americas, Asia, Europe, and Australia. The colors of the rings are (from left to right) blue, yellow, black, green, and red. At least one of these colors is on every flag of every nation in the Olympics.

The flag, however, did not appear at an Olympic Games until 1920 in Antwerp, Belgium, following World War I. It quickly became a part of the opening ceremonies. In each Olympiad since then, the flag has been handed over to the mayor of the host city by the mayor of the previous host city. It is then raised as the Olympic Hymn plays in the background. Once the games and closing ceremonies have concluded, the flag is kept in the host city's town hall until the next Olympic Games.

Passing the Torch

One year before Coubertin's death in 1937, the Berlin Organizing Committee revived the concept of an Olympic flame burning for the duration of the games. The idea derives from the ancient Greeks, who used a flame lit by the sun's rays at Olympia, the site of the original games.

Leading up to the opening ceremonies, a series of runners carry the Olympic torch into the stadium. The last runner circles the track in the stadium before igniting the Olympic flame. Symbolizing the spirit of peaceful competition, doves or pigeons are released after the lighting of the Olympic flame.

The Winter Games Are Born

The first Winter Games took place in 1924, although a few winter events had already been included in the Summer Olympics. Both the men's and women's individual skating events, as well as a pairs skating competition, were part of the 1908 Summer Games.

The first Winter Olympic Games were held in 1924. This illustration from a French journal shows some of the Summer Olympic champions from that same year.

The organizers of the 1916 Summer Games, to be held in Berlin, Germany, intended to include more Nordic events, such as cross-country skiing, but the outbreak of World War I (1914–1918) caused the games to be canceled. Winter sports did not make another appearance until the summer of 1920, when ice hockey joined the roster of events. To no one's surprise, Canada won the first gold medal in hockey.

Controversy threatened to cancel the first Winter Games even before they began. Nations in warmer climates maintained that they stood at a distinct disadvantage to nations in cold climates, where athletes had a longer training season. Scandinavian nations, such as Norway, Sweden, and Finland, feared that the Winter Olympics would detract from their own Nordic Games, which had been held in Sweden every four to five years since 1901. They refused to participate if the games were granted official status. In an attempt to appease the Scandinavians, Olympic officials agreed to call their games International Sports Week instead of the Winter Games.

Speed skaters round a bend during a race at the 1932 Winter Olympics in Lake Placid, New York.

Nordic Nations Dominate

Sixteen nations sent 258 athletes, including 13 women, to the first Winter Games held in Chamonix, France (to honor Coubertin), from January 25 to February 4, 1924. As expected, Nordic nations dominated the games. They took home 8 of the 14 gold medals offered in bobsledding, Nordic skiing, ski jumping, speed skating, figure skating, and hockey. A year later the International Olympic Committee (IOC) officially sanctioned the Winter Games, and the Chamonix games were renamed the 1924 Winter Olympics.

The 1928 Olympics at St. Moritz, Switzerland, included a number of firsts. Japan participated for the first time by sending a team of six skiers, and Germany was allowed to send a team for the first time since World War I. A new event, called the skeleton, in which athletes raced on sleds while lying flat

THE OLYMPIC IDEAL

Baron Pierre de Coubertin avidly promoted a revival of the Olympic Games because he feared sports were becoming too commercialized. He longed for a return to the Greek spirit that honored the athlete who competed for the love of sport rather than the athlete who played for money.

Coubertin expressed his views eloquently when he said, "First of all, it is necessary to maintain in sport the noble and chivalrous character which distinguished it in the past, so that it shall continue to be part of the education of present-day peoples, in the same way that sport served so wonderfully in the times of ancient Greece. The public has a tendency to transform the Olympic athlete into the paid gladiator. These two attitudes are not compatible."

on their stomachs, became part of the bobsled events. Poor weather forced some events to be cut short, and the 10,000-meter speed skating race had to be canceled because of high temperatures and melting ice.

Unfavorable weather conditions also plagued the Olympics four years later at Lake Placid, New York. Game organizers had to truck snow in so the ski jump competition could be held. The 1932 Winter Games saw the introduction of a two-man bobsled event and three demonstration sports—women's speed skating, dogsled racing, and curling. Demonstration events were not eligible for Olympic medals.

Controversy Taints the Games

American athletes won more medals than any other nation in 1932. In the friendly surroundings of Lake Placid in front of a home audience, American team members gained six gold, three silver, and two bronze medals. They captured four of the six bobsled medals by using special V-shaped runners on their sleds, which helped increase their speed.

Controversy overshadowed the speed skating events, however. European skaters had been accustomed to skating in pairs of two at a time, but at Lake Placid all skaters started together. The mass start, familiar in the United States but rarely seen in Europe, confused the athletes from overseas. As a result, the Europeans fared poorly. Afterward they complained that the unfamiliar manner of starting the races had given the United States an unfair advantage.

In the fourth Winter Olympics, a major controversy erupted that had little to do with the sporting side of the games. This time the games were held in Garmisch-Partenkirchen, Germany. When Henri de Baillet Latour, president of the International Olympic Committee, drove into Germany, he became angry over the many anti-Jewish signs placed along the roads. Signs declaring JEWS ENTER THIS PLACE AT THEIR OWN RISK and WARNING TO PICKPOCKETS AND JEWS, placed there by Adolf Hitler's Nazi Party, dotted the landscape. One day before the games were to open, Latour asked Hitler to remove the signs. When the German leader refused, Latour threatened to cancel the games and send all the athletes home. Hitler, who had been touting the importance of the games to Germany, reluctantly agreed to have the offensive signs removed.

Fortunately for the sporting world, the 1936 Winter Olympics started as scheduled with 28 nations competing. The Alpine combined, which links a downhill race with two slalom runs, made its first appearance in these games. A minor controversy marred the introduction of this event when the IOC ruled that ski instructors could not participate because they were professionals. In protest, Austrian and Swiss skiers stayed away from the games.

Olympics Surrender to World War II

World War II (1939–1945) interrupted the next two Winter Olympics, scheduled for 1940 and 1944. The IOC selected St. Moritz, Switzerland, to host the 1948 games. Switzerland had remained neutral during the war and had thereby been able to escape the devastation sustained by France, England, and other European countries. Men's and women's single slalom and downhill events were included for the first time. Today, there are five Alpine events, including the men's and women's giant slalom, introduced in 1952, and the super giant slalom, added in 1988.

Barbara Ann Scott of Canada skates before judges at the 1948 Winter Olympics. Scott won the gold medal for figure skating.

TRAINING FOR THE OLYMPICS

Before participating in the ancient Olympic Games, athletes had to first endure a rigorous 10-month training session under the supervision of special judges called *Hellanodikai.* The best in each sport were then selected to compete in the games. Judges proclaimed to the assembled hopefuls, "If you have exercised yourself in a manner worthy of the Olympic Games, if you have been guilty of no slothful or ignoble act, go on with courage. You who have not so practiced, go wither you will."

The 1948 Winter Olympics hinted at future rivalries as the Soviet Union sent observers to the games in St. Moritz, Switzerland. Since the USSR was not affiliated with the IOC, Soviet athletes did not compete in the Olympics until 1956.

Four years later, the Winter Games were staged in a Scandinavian nation for the first time. Oslo, Norway, was selected as the host city. The two major defeated powers in World War II, Germany and Japan, who had been barred from the 1948 games, once again took part. New events included two Nordic competitions, a 10-kilometer cross-country race for women, and giant slalom races for men and women.

When Soviet men and women joined the games in 1956, they quickly showed their athletic excellence in many events. It was the beginning of the medals race between the United States and the Soviet Union that would last for decades. The Soviet Union sent its first team to the 1956 games in Cortina d'Ampezzo, Italy. The talented team won more medals than any other nation, surpassing Scandinavian nations in Nordic events and trouncing every opponent in hockey. For the first time, live television captured the drama of the games when an Italian television station broadcast from the site.

South Africa sent athletes to the Winter Games for the first time in 1960 in Squaw Valley, California. Their participation proved short-lived, however. Before the 1964 games, Olympic officials had barred the nation from sending a delegation because of its segregationist policy, called apartheid, which deprived black South Africans of their civil rights. (The ban was lifted in time for the 1994 games, after a change of government in South Africa ended apartheid.) Women's speed skating and the biathlon debuted in the 1960 games, while the bobsledding competition had to be dropped when officials declared the course unfit for use.

More than 1,000 athletes attended the 1964 Winter Games in Innsbruck, Austria. The luge was added as an event, and a 70-meter ski jumping competition joined the Nordic skiing lineup. The games were hampered by poor weather when rising temperatures melted much of the snow. Conditions on the ski slopes and other venues were far from satisfactory and may have contributed to the deaths of two athletes—an Australian skier and a British bobsled racer—during practice runs.

The 1968 games in Grenoble, France, foreshadowed the struggles between the International Olympic Committee and the competitors. The first hint of the brewing storm occurred when the president of the IOC, Avery Brundage, threatened to cancel the skiing events unless athletes removed the manufacturers' labels on their equipment. Although he temporarily backed away from this rigid position, he had laid the foundation for a more explosive incident, which occurred during the next Olympics.

IOC Gets Tough

At the 1972 games in Sapporo, Japan, Canadian ice hockey officials contended that the state-supported Eastern European teams were actually professionals competing as amateurs. They demanded that Canada be allowed to send its best athletes, which in this case meant players from the professional National Hockey League. Olympic officials denied their request, so the Canadian team stayed home.

IOC president Avery Brundage, who believed the Olympic spirit of amateurism was being destroyed by what he saw as a dangerous union of athletes and manufacturers, banned Austrian ski hero Karl Schranz three days before the games opened. Many athletes, including Schranz, had received payments from companies whose equipment they used, but Brundage chose to make an example of Schranz because the skier had been so outspoken in his criticism of the IOC president. Though some Olympians threatened to boycott, the games proceeded without interruption—and without Schranz.

The 1976 Winter Olympics introduced another heated issue. At first the Olympic committee selected Denver, Colorado, to host the games, but citizens' groups in Colorado objected on the grounds that the competition would disrupt the natural habitat of animals and harm the environment. They expressed their displeasure even more strongly by approving a law that prohibited the use of tax dollars for any event that threatened the environment. The IOC turned to Austria to stage the games. Though the affair threw the Winter Olympics into momentary confusion, the issue of protecting the environment was here to stay. Future organizers

TORCH RELAY

The first torch relay in the Winter Olympics occurred in 1952 at the Winter Games in Oslo, Norway. To celebrate such an important athletic event in a Scandinavian nation, Norway organized an impressive ceremony. The Olympic flame was kindled at the home of skier Sondre Nordheim, one of the country's most famous athletes, then relayed by a succession of 94 skiers to Oslo's Bislett Stadium for the opening ceremony.

A MORE DEMOCRATIC OLYMPICS

In the past, when athletes had to pay for their own training and equipment, Olympians tended to come from wealthier families. By 1998 the Olympic Games had become a more democratic institution, open to any competitor. Since Olympic officials now permit more financial support from nations, any talented athlete can try out for the Olympic dream.

made sure to consider environmental concerns when constructing the courses for the events.

A second boycott by athletes occurred in 1980 at the games in the island nation of Taiwan. Off the eastern coast of mainland China, Taiwan has long proclaimed itself the legitimate government of China. When the IOC ruled that Taiwan could not call itself the "Republic of China," its athletes stayed home.

A New Direction

The International Olympic Committee dramatically altered the Olympic schedule in 1986 when it decided to alternate the Winter and Summer Olympics every two years. Up to that point, the Winter Games had been held in the same year as the Summer Games, but that left a four-year gap between games. The IOC believed that staging a contest every two years would create greater public interest. Many nations had also expressed concerns about the difficulty of organizing and sending two Olympic teams into competition in the same year.

The number of Alpine and Nordic skiing events increased at the 1988 games in Calgary, Canada. Men's and women's super giant slaloms debuted in Calgary, while the men's and women's Alpine combined returned after a 36-year absence. In Nordic skiing, a ski jumping team and Nordic combined team also made the roster. Three demonstration sports were introduced at Calgary: freestyle skiing, short track speed skating, and curling. While these games were the last for athletes from the former Soviet Union, which was about to dissolve, they were the first opportunity for a team of bobsledders from Jamaica.

The End of the Cold War

The 1992 games in Albertville, France, were memorable because, for the first time, the once-dominant East German and Soviet teams no longer existed. Political unrest had toppled communist governments in both countries and sent their athletic programs into disarray. Instead of two separate teams representing East and West Germany, a united Germany sent one team, while the former Soviet Union formed a five-state alliance that included Russia, Ukraine, and three other former communist states. With the Cold War era ending, athletes could forget politics and focus on competing for the honor of appearing in the games.

Men's and women's short track speed skating, a women's biathlon, and freestyle skiing made their first appearances in the 1992 games. Freestyle skiing offered men's and women's mogul competitions, and two years later men's and women's freestyle aerials were added as medal events at Lillehammer, Norway.

At the 1998 games held in Nagano, Japan, women's hockey became an Olympic sport. The United States and Canada squared off in a memorable gold medal game. Behind the goaltending of Sara Tuetny and the offensive prowess of Sandra Whyte, the United States won a 3-1 decision and took home the gold medal. Snowboarding also made its debut as an Olympic sport and was very popular among spectators.

Salt Lake City, Utah, will host the 2002 Winter Games from February 8 through February 24. The Salt Lake City games are expected to be the largest Winter Games ever, with more than 3,500 athletes and officials from about 80 countries.

Members of the United States women's hockey team celebrate after winning gold at the 1998 Winter Olympics in Nagano, Japan.

ALPINE SKIING

Alpine refers to the Alps, the majestic mountain range in central Europe where downhill skiing originated. Alpine skiing consists of five different downhill races that combine speed, balance, and daring. Athletes must constantly be on guard for a sudden curve or drop that could spiral them off course as they zoom down the treacherous courses, which are set up on steep, bumpy slopes. Alpine skiing is a favorite among spectators; in Europe, downhill racers are treated like superstars.

THE HISTORY OF SKIING

Skiing originated thousands of years ago in northern regions of Europe and Asia. Perhaps the earliest depiction of a person on skis is a Scandinavian drawing dating to 5000 B.C. The oldest known ski, believed to be 5,000 years old, is housed in the Djugarden Museum in Stockholm, Sweden. Skis were used by the Russian Army in 1483 and came into widespread use in Europe shortly afterward.

Early ski poles were simply sturdy tree branches. Eventually, pieces of bone were attached to the ends of the sticks. The sharp, durable bone fragments enabled skiers to dig the poles into the snow and propel themselves forward. The first recorded mention of the use of two ski poles occurs in a Finnish story dating from 1615.

Origin of the Sport

Austrians, living amid rugged mountains, gained a reputation as great skiers as early as the 1700s. One writer noted that Austrian skiers moved across snow country on five-foot skis so naturally that "no mountain is too steep, or too overgrown with big trees to prevent them skiing down it; they wind and twist about like a snake. But if the terrain is open they run straight, leaning back on their sticks, firmly and stiffly as if they had no limbs or joints in their bodies."

In North America, Eskimos and Greenlanders were the first to take up skiing in the early 1700s. In 1759, a skiing contest was the main attraction at a Canadian ice festival.

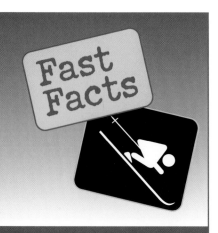

Fast Facts

First Olympic competition

Garmisch-Partenkirchen, Germany; 1936

Legendary athletes

Jean-Claude Killy, **France**
Andrea Mead Lawrence, **USA**
Hermann Maier, **Austria**
Toni Sailer, **Austria**
Ingemar Stenmark, **Sweden**
Picabo Street, **USA**
Alberto Tomba, **Italy**

Criteria for winning

Fastest time

The world's first ski competition took place among Norwegian soldiers in 1767, and the first ski club was organized in Christiania (now Oslo), Norway, in 1870. Norwegian athletes perfected downhill skiing. They introduced the sport in Germany, Austria, and Switzerland, where they found the deep snows and perilous slopes of the Alps to be a perfect setting. Since the late 1800s, downhill skiing has been immensely popular in those countries.

American skiers slowly developed an interest in the sport. In the first recorded ski race in 1854 in Sierra County, California, competitors used 15-foot (4.6-meter) skis to race straight downhill for a silver trophy. Two decades later, dozens of downhill events were being organized in the California mountains. In 1904, skiing enthusiasts gathered at Ishpeming, Michigan, to form the National Ski Association, and the first American ski school opened at Peckett's Inn on Sugar Hill in the mountains surrounding Franconia, New Hampshire.

Two Austrians, Mathias Zdarsky and Hannes Schneider, were responsible for developing techniques that improved skiers' abilities to control their speed, turning, and stopping. Zdarsky, considered by most ski historians as the father of Alpine skiing, showed how to push one ski at an angle to the fall line and keep the weight of the upper body tilted forward. In this way, the skier is able to achieve greater balance. This technique forms the basis of modern skiing methods.

In the late 1800s, Henry Lunn started the Public Schools Alpine Sports Club to promote Alpine skiing in England. In 1911 he organized the first downhill race, called the Roberts of Kandahar Challenge. Eleven years later his son, Arnold Lunn, staged the world's first modern slalom in Switzerland. (The word *slalom* means "turning.") The first Winter Olympics featured the downhill, and the World Ski Championships were initiated the following year.

A revolutionary idea in the 1930s attracted thousands of people worldwide to the sport of skiing. Resorts began to construct ski lifts, which enabled ski buffs to use the slopes easily and inexpensively. Today more than 1,000 ski resorts accommodate the millions of Americans who have taken up recreational skiing.

American soldiers returning home after World War II played a large role in popularizing skiing in the United States. Some had served in the special mountain units, where skis were part of their equipment, while others had learned to ski during their tours of duty in France, Italy, Germany, and other parts of central Europe.

Austrian skier Toni Sailer, who won three gold medals at the 1956 Olympics in Cortina d'Ampezzo, Italy, explained the allure of Alpine skiing. According to Sailer, skiing is the "most thrilling, yet most relaxing, and the healthiest [sport]. It combines the open air pleasure of golfing or mountain climbing, the powerful precision of tennis, and the elegance of figure skating." Sailer added, "Skiing is more than just a sport, it's a way of life, an addiction."

Competing in the Event

Alpine skiers use the tucked position, shown here, to decrease wind resistance and gain speed.

Equipment for Alpine skiing is similar to that used in other forms of skiing, except the skis, boots, and bindings are designed to allow greater control and quicker release in case of a fall. Alpine skis are made of thin strips of wood, metal, or other material, and they curve up at the front end. To make turns easier, the center of the ski, called the midbody, is slightly raised above the level of the tip and the tail. The skis also have metal edges along both sides for more control in turns. Athletes apply special waxes to their skis to produce higher speeds as they race across the snow. The lengths of the skis vary depending on the height of the athlete. Downhill skis are shorter and wider than those used in the Nordic events, and they usually measure 6 to 7 feet (1.8 to 2.1 meters) in length.

Ski boots made from plastic or hard leather cover and support the ankles. Ski bindings hold the boots to the skis. To avoid serious injuries during spills, the ski bindings release the skis whenever the athlete falls.

To increase speed, improve balance, and aid direction, the athlete uses ski poles made of fiberglass, aluminum, steel, or bamboo. The ski poles end in a sharp point surrounded by a circular webbed ring called the basket, which prevents the pole from sinking deep into the snow. Skiers hold a rubber or plastic handle at the top of the pole called the grip.

Alpine skiers wear warmer clothing than cross-country skiers because their races are shorter and they have less time to produce body heat. Over thermal underwear, the Alpine skier typically wears a turtleneck sweater, insulated ski pants, a parka (or a snowsuit), plus gloves and a hat.

Five different events comprise Alpine skiing for both men and women: the downhill, slalom, giant slalom, super giant slalom (nicknamed the super-G), and the combined (slalom and downhill). Competitors ski down the slope once in the downhill and super giant slalom, while they make two runs in the other three events.

The downhill and the super giant slalom demand speed, while the shorter slalom and giant slalom require skilled body control to maneuver through gates. Usually, athletes compete in either the speed or the technical events, although some have participated in both.

The top 15 seeded athletes ski before the other competitors, which gives them the advantage of skiing on a fresh course. Most prefer to jump off from somewhere between the fifth and tenth spot, however, so they can follow their predecessors' trails. In deteriorating weather conditions, the lower-ranked skiers run down first to create a better trail for the top seeds.

Courses vary depending on the contours of the hills being used, but they generally conform to certain standards.

Officials inspect the courses to ensure there is sufficient snow cover on the slopes, the snow is smooth, small obstacles have been removed, all gates are secure, and proper safety nets or padding have been placed in the more dangerous areas.

All courses have a starting area that is roped off for the competitors; a starting gate made of two poles 29.5 inches (75 centimeters) apart; the winding course with gates; and a finishing area of smoothly packed snow banked by snow walls, foam rubber, or other protective material to prevent the skier from colliding with anything dangerous at the bottom of the run. The finish line is marked by two posts connected at the top by a large banner.

Before each race or practice, two professional skiers called forerunners ski the course to check the conditions. They also create a path for the other athletes to follow, if they so choose.

Slalom is set up on a course with a vertical drop of between 459–722 feet (140 and 220 meters) for men and 393–591 feet (120 and 180 meters) for women. There are 55 to 75 gates for men and 40 to 60 gates for women. Gates are placed at varying intervals and combinations to test the athlete's ability to maneuver between them. Each skier must pass between all the gates in proper order to avoid disqualification. If a gate is missed, the racer must turn back and pass through it before continuing to the finish. This, of course, adds time to the racer's run and may cost the athlete several places in the standings. The giant slalom is similar to the slalom except that it is run on a steeper, faster course that demands greater expertise.

Downhill racing, the ultimate speed skiing event, is held on a course with at least a 2,500-foot vertical drop. While skiers may select their own path down the steep slope, they must pass through all the designated control gates—parallel poles with flags attached. Doing so steers skiers away from dangerous locations, but also forces them to slow down momentarily. Top skiers can finish the course in fewer than 2 minutes and attain speeds approaching 70 to 80 miles per hour (130 to 148 kilometers per hour). The competitor with the shortest time completing the course wins the event.

The ideal downhill skier has muscular thighs and buttocks to absorb the numerous shocks created by the bumpy courses, and narrow shoulders and upper arms to diminish wind resistance. Skiers crouch low to the ground with their chests close to their knees to reduce air resistance. Since hitting bumps tends to elevate the skier into the air and add to the actual distance traveled, skiers like to pull their skis off the snow as they approach the bumps.

Athletes in the downhill use three basic movements—schussing, traversing, and turning. The skier prefers schussing, which means skiing in as straight a path as possible to increase speed. Whenever the athlete needs to control speed, he or she skis at an angle to the slopes. This is called traversing. The skier turns by either holding the ski tips together in the shape of a wedge or by holding the skis parallel and leaning left or right.

Athletes agree that the downhill provides the most thrilling challenges for skiers. French athlete JEAN-CLAUDE KILLY described the downhill as the toughest race because it "tests character and courage." His fellow countryman Guy Périllat said, "The downhill does not leave room for compromise. You're either in front, or you perish." One of the great Austrian skiers, Karl Schranz, added, "The downhill demands everything a skier is able to give. No coward will ever win."

The super giant slalom, known as the super-G, combines the downhill and giant slalom. Athletes compete in one run down a course that features numerous gates and demands high speeds. Once out of the starting gate, the athlete zooms down the hill, ignoring the dangers and focusing only on gaining speed, all to the delight of the spectators. American skier Diann Roffe-Steinrotter, a gold and silver medalist, summed it up best when she said, "It's one day, one hill, one and a half minutes, and whoever shakes and bakes the best is going to get the gold."

Injuries are common in downhill. Austrian skier HERMANN MAIER won the gold medal in 1998 at Nagano, Japan, but not without having the scare of his life. He lost control on one of his runs, flew through the air, and crashed through two safety fences. Maier emerged unharmed, unlike two-time Olympic downhiller Chad Fleischer from Vail, Colorado.

FROM CONTENDER TO SPECTATOR

Heading into the 1998 Winter Games at Nagano, Japan, one of Canada's top prospects in the downhill was Cary Mullen—that is, until an injury removed him from consideration. At a race at Beaver Creek, Colorado, Mullen lost control in the final stretch and smashed his head on a hard surface. The unconscious athlete tumbled more than 100 yards before coming to a stop just short of the finish line. For several months a severe concussion gave Mullen double vision, and although his vision returned to normal just before the Nagano Games, he missed making the Canadian team. Nonetheless, Mullen traveled to Japan to cheer on his friends. Asked by a reporter how he felt, Mullen smiled and replied, "I'm just glad to see *one* of you."

Fleischer dislocated his left shoulder during a December 1999 event in Italy, forcing him to sit out the rest of the season. He was philosophical, however: "It's better now than in 2002, when there's Olympic gold to be won. This is just part of the sport, as anyone else like A.J. [Kitt], Tommy [Moe], or Picabo [Street] will tell you. It's just a minor setback. I've got to keep my eye on the big picture, which is to be healthy."

After the Olympic medals, Alpine skiing's most coveted trophy is the World Cup title, which is awarded each year to the man and woman who earn the most points in World Cup competition. The World Cup races are held in Europe and North America during the winter months, with athletes earning points for finishing among the top contestants. Skiers also look to the World Ski Championships, held every odd-numbered year.

Maneuvering past a gate, an Alpine skier races toward the finish line during the men's giant slalom competition at the 1998 Winter Olympics.

In the Olympics

The first of the Alpine events—the men's and women's combined—made their appearance at the 1936 Winter Games held in Garmisch-Partenkirchen, Germany. To dictator Adolf Hitler's joy, German athletes took the gold and silver medals in both events. Twelve years later, at the games in St. Moritz, Switzerland, the men's and women's downhill and slalom events were included, followed by the giant slalom in 1952 and the super-G in 1988.

American women made a name for themselves early on. In 1948, Gretchen Fraser captured the gold in the slalom and a silver in the combined, and four years later ANDREA MEAD LAWRENCE took home gold medals in both the slalom and the giant slalom.

Antoin Miliordos of Greece established an unwanted record in the slalom by falling 18 times during one of his runs in the 1952 games and posting a time that was 26.9 seconds slower than the total of both runs of gold medal winner Othmar Schneider of Austria. Angry and embarrassed over his dismal performance, Miliordos sat down and crossed the finish line backwards.

One of the big stories in 1952 was the weather. A lack of snowfall forced workers to haul snow from higher altitudes and pack it onto the courses, but this made for uneven surfaces that tripped many skiers. A steady string of athletes entered the Olympic hospital even before the games started. Fearing what lay ahead, a French official warned, "The Olympic downhill ski competition will be a race to death if it doesn't snow soon." Japanese skiers labeled the run "a hara-kiri [suicide] with a run-on." Concern eased when more than 14 inches of snow fell before the event. But then a sudden thaw melted much of the snow and created treacherous, icy conditions.

Austria's Toni Sailer swept all three Alpine events in 1956 (downhill, slalom, and giant slalom). Called the "Blitz from Kitz" for his hometown of Kitzbuhel, Sailer skied before he was out of diapers. He described his first ski outing in his memoirs: "My father bundled me and a pair of tiny skis and poles and we went to a test hill behind our home in Kitzbuhel. There, he put us together and, after a countdown that included fixing of diapers, he shoved me down the hill." The little skier fell dozens of times, but he was hooked.

Sailer called the downhill his favorite because, unlike a slalom where the skier has to slow for turns, the downhill allowed him to focus on speed: "I like to run free. The secret of downhill is really the ability to think ahead."

Moments before the 1956 event, one of the straps holding Sailer's boot to the ski broke when he tried to tighten it. Since this had never happened before, Sailer had not thought to bring an extra strap. If he could not find a substitute, he would have to withdraw from the event. Fortunately Hansi Senger, the trainer for the Italian team, walked by, saw Sailer's predicament, and gave the Austrian the straps from his own skis. Sailer swept to victory down a course that sent eight competitors to the hospital.

Two years later, Sailer's countrymen voted him the fifth most influential person in Austrian history, just behind the famed musician Wolfgang Amadeus Mozart. In the 1970s, Sailer was appointed head coach of a demoralized Austrian ski team and succeeded in turning it around.

The United States men's team emerged from years of frustration when two of its members won Alpine medals in 1964 at Innsbruck, Austria. Billy Kidd's silver and Jimmy Heuga's bronze medal meant that the Americans were finally contenders in the slalom. The downhill event that year showed that while the sport brought gold and glory, it could also exact a terrible toll. American skier Buddy Werner once said, "If you want to be first, you have to take chances. There are only two places in a race—first and last." Ross Milne of Australia took chances and paid the harshest price. Milne died after losing control and crashing into a tree during practice for the downhill.

In 1968, dashing French skier Jean-Claude Killy matched Toni Sailer's feat by taking three gold medals at Grenoble, France. In his first event, Killy, who put on his first pair of skis at age three, won the downhill by a mere .08 seconds, but the victory energized the French skier: "Winning the downhill gave me confidence and took some of the pressure off. So, in the giant slalom, I hardly had the feeling that I was racing in the Olympics at all."

After winning a second gold medal in the giant slalom, Killy followed with a win in the slalom. Controversy surrounded the event, however. Killy's main rival, Austrian skier Karl Schranz, had to halt his run as he approached the 22nd gate because an unidentified individual dressed in black crossed in front of him. Schranz returned to the starting gate, where officials allowed him to start again. This time, Schranz skied a perfect run and took first place. Two hours later, however, officials disqualified Schranz for missing two gates prior to the encounter with the mysterious intruder.

Schranz countered by saying that if he missed any gates, he did so because of the man in black. He and his Austrian teammates wondered if the man had been a French police officer or soldier who purposely tried to distract the Austrian so that Killy could win his third medal. The French team responded by accusing Schranz of making up the story to hide the fact that he had missed a gate. A five-judge panel ruled 3-2 against Schranz and awarded the gold medal to Killy. Following his triple triumph, Killy, who was adored by women around the world for his captivating smile, movie-star looks, and daring speed on the slopes, retired from competitive skiing.

Austrian skiers again dominated the sports headlines in the 1970s. Karl Schranz made news off the slopes when the longtime head of the International Olympic Committee, Avery Brundage, challenged the skier's amateur status. In a controversial ruling, Brundage persuaded the Olympic Committee to ban Schranz from participating in the 1972 games because he had allowed his name and picture to be used in advertisements. It was the second Olympics in a row in which Schranz found himself at the center of controversy.

Austria's Franz Klammer, known as the "Austrian Astronaut," erased the memory of the Schranz affair four years later by skiing one of the most amazing downhill runs at the 1976 games in Innsbruck, Austria. A speedy showing by Olympic favorite Bernhard Russi had put him in a comfortable position for the gold, but Franz Klammer—to the delight of 60,000 Austrian spectators—bounded down the slopes with total abandon. Late in the run he went into a deep crouch position in an effort to make up time. While the crouch reduces air resistance, the move also makes it much harder for the athlete to control his skis. Ignoring danger on every bump, Klammer swept past the finishing gate to win first place by four-tenths of a second. An excited Klammer later told reporters, "I thought I was going to crash all the way. Now I've got everything. I don't need anything else."

Klammer achieved something else, though, winning ten consecutive downhill races, including the Olympic gold, between January 1976 and January 1977. After winning his

"GO, HERBIE, GO!"

Athletes sometimes find inspiration in unusual places. In the 1972 games at Sapporo, Japan, Swiss skier Marie-Theres Nadig claimed a gold medal in the women's downhill, a feat she later attributed partly to a silly movie called *The Love Bug*. As she neared the end of the race, Nadig suddenly thought of the movie about a Volkswagen that entered Grand Prix automobile races. As she told *Ski* magazine, "The little car was called Herbie. In each race, it would start ahead of the other champions who would chase it. Suddenly I saw myself in the role of Herbie. I was being chased by hordes of other racers. A voice inside me said, 'Go, Herbie, go, go, go.' At each 'go,' I would lower my body still further to cut the wind resistance. In my whole life I never skied in such a low crouch. I could have easily fallen. But inside me, I always heard the voice crying out, 'Go, Herbie, go.'"

fifth World Cup downhill title in 1983, Klammer continued skiing until the 1984 Olympic Games in Sarajevo, Yugoslavia, where he finished a poor tenth in the downhill.

At the same games, Rosi Mittermaier of West Germany barely missed taking three gold medals. After winning the downhill and the slalom, she finished second in the giant slalom by only 0.12 seconds.

Though INGEMAR STENMARK had won gold medals in the slalom and giant slalom in 1980, he was bested in the medal count by female skier Hanni Wenzel. Wenzel, from the tiny European nation of Liechtenstein, won two gold medals in the slalom and giant slalom and a silver in the downhill.

An Italian skier, ALBERTO TOMBA, dominated Olympic headlines in the 1980s and 1990s. The daring skier, nicknamed "La Bomba," thrilled spectators with the bold and almost reckless way he attacked the slopes. His audacity paid off with gold medals in the slalom and giant slalom in 1988, and gold and silver medals in the 1994 Winter Games. Another of Alpine skiing's greats, Ingemar Stenmark, commented that Tomba "may be the greatest slalom skier ever."

At the same time that Tomba was number one in men's skiing, female skier Vreni Schneider from Switzerland made Olympic history in women's events. The athlete, who first skied at age three, won five medals, including three gold, in different Olympics. No other female athlete has matched this achievement in Alpine skiing.

While American skiers performed poorly in Alpine events in the first 40 years of Olympic competition, they have made their presence felt in recent games. Bill Johnson won a gold medal in the downhill in 1984, while brothers Phil and Steve Mahre took gold and silver medals in the slalom. The Mahres showed great skill on the demanding course that took out half of the contenders. Seven of the top 15 competitors either crashed or missed gates and were disqualified. Phil Mahre, World Cup champion in 1981, 1982, and 1983, had also won a silver medal during the 1980 games, even though he skied with a 3-inch metal plate and four screws in his left ankle because of a serious injury suffered a year earlier.

Few Americans were as successful as Tommy Moe. Though he had never won a World Cup race, Moe grabbed a gold medal in the downhill event, then added a silver in the super-G at Lillehammer, Norway, in 1994. Undisciplined early in his career, Moe credits his father, Tommy Moe, Sr., with giving him a focus that enabled him to succeed in the Olympics. In 1986, when Moe was kicked off the United States team for smoking marijuana, his father brought Moe to the lonely Alaskan camp where he worked. The younger Moe worked 12-hour days as a laborer, and admits now that while his Alaskan adventure was difficult, "it humbled me pretty fast."

With each passing year, Moe steadily improved on the World Cup tour. It was his performance at Lillehammer, however, that caught everyone's attention. Moe became the first American male skier to win two Alpine medals in the same Olympics.

The world becomes a blur as Alpine skiers reach speeds of more than 75 miles per hour.

On the women's side, American skier PICABO STREET rivaled Moe for publicity and flashiness. In 1995 she became the first American to win a World Cup title. Her second title followed in 1996. Street was dropped from the 1990 United States team for lacking discipline, but she worked hard and regained her position on the team the next year. In 1994, she skied to a silver medal in the downhill and added a gold medal in the same event in 1998.

The upbeat Street did not dwell on the dangers inherent to her sport, preferring instead to focus on doing well: "I love what I'm doing. For so many ski racers, competition becomes a job. If it does, you'll never be great at it. For me, the World Cup circuit is so much fun; I love the day-in and day-out—seeing everyone go through changes, going through changes myself, making new friends, learning new languages."

Norway's Kjetil Andre Aamodt showed versatility in the 1990s by winning Olympic medals in four of the five Alpine events. In 1992, he earned a gold medal in the super-G and a bronze in the giant slalom. Two years later he added two silvers in the combined and the downhill, and a bronze in the super-G.

Austria's Hermann Maier experienced joy and suffering during the 1998 Games at Nagano, Japan. Called by fans "Das Munster" (The Monster) and the "Herminator," the powerful skier won gold medals in the giant slalom and the slalom. In between the two events, he finished out of the running in the downhill when he lost control on a turn, flew 30 yards (27.4 meters) through the air, and crashed through two safety nets. Fourteen other

Many competitors agree that the downhill provides the most thrilling challenges for skiers.

skiers also crashed on the treacherous downhill course, including Italian Luca Cattaneo, who had to be airlifted to a hospital. "It was chaos," said Maier. "It was too difficult. I've never seen anything like it."

Alberto Tomba made a miserable exit at the Nagano Games. The gifted Italian superstar hoped to finish his career with another medal, which would make him the first Alpine skier to win a medal in four successive Winter Games, but fate was against him. He crashed only 18 seconds into his run in the giant slalom and injured his groin. Two days later he tried to race in the slalom, but dropped out after a slow first run put him in 17th place.

Tomba recalled that in the 1993 World Championships, which had also been held in Japan, he slid off the course in the slalom and missed the giant slalom because of food poisoning. "Japan doesn't bring me much luck. I've always failed here," Tomba noted with disappointment.

BIATHLON

The biathlon requires athletes to master two seemingly contrasting skills—speed on skis for the cross-country portion of the event, and calmness and accuracy for the rifle shooting portion. Biathlons have long been popular in the Scandinavian countries and in Germany and Russia.

◀ **SEE HISTORY OF SKIING ON PAGE 18.**

Origin of the Sport

During World War II (1939–1945), Finnish soldiers on skis fought off the invading Soviet army and vanished into the snowy forests. American ski troops, all in white, defeated the Germans in Italy's rugged mountains. When they returned home after the war, they introduced cross-country skiing and the biathlon to America.

Although Norway organized biathlon competitions as early as 1776, the biathlon did not become an international sport until 1957, one year before the first world championship was held. From its humble beginnings, the biathlon has expanded to include participants from most continents. Technological improvements, such as replacing the cumbersome army rifle with a lighter, smaller bore (barrel) rifle in 1977, helped popularize the sport, as did the introduction of television coverage of the Olympics.

Competing in the Event

The Olympic biathlon offers a unique challenge. The first part of the event requires that the competitor race to the firing zone, an activity that elevates the heart rate. Once in the firing zone, the athlete needs a steady hand to accurately shoot at the targets. This means that the athlete must ski as fast as possible without elevating the heart rate to a level that interferes with marksmanship. Only through proper training and superb physical conditioning can athletes master these dual challenges.

The course is similar for all biathlon events. It begins on a straightaway with two separate tracks that blend into one in

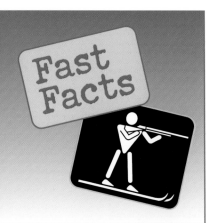

Fast Facts

First Olympic competition

Men's
Squaw Valley, California; 1960

Women's
Albertville, France; 1992

Legendary athletes

Myriam Bédard, Canada

Mark Kirchner, Germany

Frank-Peter Roetsch, East Germany

Criteria for winning

Fastest time

the middle section, and finishes on another straightaway. Most of the course is laid out over hilly terrain to further challenge the athletes. Approximately one-third of the course runs over flat terrain, one-third rises uphill, and one-third descends. The highest point does not exceed 5,414 feet (1,650 meters), and the final portion is double-tracked so that opponents can race head-to-head.

The clothing worn by skiers varies, but it may not exceed roughly one-quarter inch in thickness. Most competitors wear thermal underwear and long wool hose, knee breeches, shirt, sweater, insulated parka, goggles, hat or headband, and gloves.

The boots are made of plastic or lightweight leather to cover and support the ankles. Special ski bindings fasten the boots to the skis, securing only the front portion of the boot so the skier can easily lift his heel as he moves. Athletes also use ski poles made of fiberglass, aluminum, steel, or bamboo to provide speed and balance and to increase steering ability.

The skis, typically made from fiberglass, hardwood, or aluminum, curve slightly upward at the tip for ease of motion across the surface of the snow. They must be a minimum of 1.6 inches (4 centimeters) less than the height of the athlete, and they must weigh less than 26.3 pounds (750 grams).

After skiing over hilly terrain to reach the firing zone, biathletes fire their rifles from the prone position.

A single-loading .22-caliber rifle is used in target shooting. The rifles must weigh at least 7.5 pounds, and the sights cannot contain magnifying devices.

In the Olympics

The Winter Olympics offers three biathlon events for both men and women. The shorter races are called the sprints and consist of the men's 10-kilometer (6.2-mile) and the women's 7.5-kilometer (4.6-mile). Athletes stop twice during the race to fire at targets, once while lying on their stomachs in the snow (prone position) and once standing up.

Longer races offer a more rigorous challenge. Called individual events, these races cover 20 kilometers (12 miles) for men and 15 kilometers (9 miles) for women. The competitors shoot four different times, twice from a prone position and twice from a standing position.

Competitors are organized into four groups. Team captains select the order in which their athletes compete, but each nation is allowed no more than one entrant per group. For both the individual and sprint events, athletes leave the starting gate one at a time exactly one minute apart. A mass start, in which all skiers begin at the same time, is used in the relay races.

The cross-country portion of the biathlon, shown here, requires great strength and stamina.

Biathletes ski to the first firing zone, load five rounds into their rifle, shoot at the targets, and then ski to the next zone. Alternately shooting from a prone position in one zone and a standing position in the other, each contestant fires at five black dots spread out horizontally on a white target 55 yards (50 meters) away. For the prone position, the targets are 4.5 centimeters in diameter, about the size of a silver dollar. For the standing position, the targets are 11.5 centimeters in diameter, the size of a softball. For optimum accuracy, the athletes attempt to shoot during the interval between heartbeats when they are calmest.

When shooting in the prone position, competitors may support the rifle only with their hands, and they must unload their rifles after each round. Athletes incur penalties for missing a target. In the individual event each miss adds one minute to the competitor's final time, while athletes in the sprint events must ski a 164-yd (150-m) penalty loop for each miss. The athlete whose total time, adjusted for any penalties, is the lowest wins.

In the biathlon relay, each skier (four for the men's event and three for the women's) races 4.7 miles (7.5 km) and stops twice to fire up to eight shots at the five targets. The athlete may carry only five bullets in the rifle's magazine, and if he or she has not hit all five targets by the time the magazine is empty, the biathlete may use the extra three bullets. The competitor must open the bolt of the rifle for each extra bullet, load it, fire, remove the spent shell, and load the next bullet. Since this requires additional time, teams hope to hit each target with the first five bullets.

The relay begins with a mass start instead of an individual start. At the end of each leg, the athlete enters the passover zone. This is a 22-yd (20-m) section where the competitor must touch his or her teammate's body with the hand to initiate their start.

The biathlon first appeared in the 1960 Winter Olympics with the introduction of the men's 20-kilometer at Squaw Valley, California. Eight years later the men's relay was added, and at the 1980 Winter Olympics in Lake Placid, New York, the men's 10-kilometer event made its debut. All three women's biathlon events were finally introduced in the 1992 Olympic Games at Albertville, France.

RULES FOR DISQUALIFICATION

Biathletes not only have to worry about weather conditions, opponents, and coming through under pressure, but they also face an imposing list of infractions that could disqualify them from competition. A few actions that can result in such a penalty are

- firing more than the set number of shots at the target

- remaining in an incorrect firing position after being warned

- firing unauthorized sighting shots

- making alterations to equipment after the start of the race

- changing the weapon after the start of the race

The first Olympic biathlon clearly demonstrated that an equal blend of the two skills of skiing and shooting is crucial to winning the race. Victor Arbez of France easily outraced every competitor in the 20-kilometer event, but along the way he missed 18 of his 20 targets. This added an extra 36 minutes to his total (athletes incurred a two-minute penalty for each missed shot in 1960) and plunged the Frenchman to a distant 25th place overall.

Klas Lestander of Sweden skied 8 minutes slower than Arbenz and 14 other competitors, but because he was the only biathlete to hit all 20 targets and avoid penalty minutes, he posted the lowest adjusted time and captured the gold medal. The silver medalist, Antti Tyrväinen of Finland, completed the course 3.5 minutes faster than Lestander, but his two missed shots cost him 4 penalty minutes. The Finn lost the gold medal by only 36 seconds of adjusted time.

In the 1988 games in Calgary, Canada, East German biathlete FRANK-PETER ROETSCH became the first athlete to win gold medals in both the 10-kilometer and 20-kilometer events. Four years later at Albertville, Mark Kirchner of Germany won gold medals in the 10-kilometer and relay events and a silver medal in the 20-kilometer individual.

One of the greatest female biathletes to take part in the Winter Olympics swept to fame in the 1994 games at Lillehammer, Norway. Myriam Bédard of Canada grew up near Quebec. After training as a figure skater, Bédard switched to the biathlon as a teenager. The intense training regimen, which often demanded that the athlete work alone, appealed to the quiet young woman, and by the time Bédard was 15, she had already won her first race. She raced to victory in borrowed ski boots that were so large that she had to stuff tissue into the toes to make them fit.

Within a year Bédard had captured the Canadian junior championships, posing a serious threat to European domination of the Olympics. In 1992 she surprised observers by earning a bronze medal in the 15-kilometer, but poor performances in 1993 cast doubt on her ability to maintain the pace.

Bédard proved her critics wrong with her showing at Lillehammer, Norway, in 1994. Pitted against stiff competition from Germany's Uschi Disl, France's Anne Briand Bouthiaux, and biathletes from the former Soviet Union, Bédard crushed the field in the 15-kilometer with a winning margin of 46.7 seconds. She followed her feat by taking a gold medal in the 7.5-kilometer competition, this time by the razor-thin margin of 1.1 seconds.

Bédard later learned that she had skied on a mismatched pair of skis in the 7.5-kilometer race. Though minor, the mix-up almost cost her the gold medal. She recalled the incident: "I had one ski that was gliding more. All through the race, the right one was going good and the left one was going bad. It's funny now because I won. But if I had not won, you'd think about that all your life—one second."

Bédard became a national hero in Canada. Her stunning success in the sport helped popularize the biathlon, which until that time had been overshadowed in North America by hockey, figure skating, and skiing.

One of the most notable Americans in the biathlon is Lyle Nelson. His 19th-place finish in the men's 10-kilometer event in Nagano, Japan, in 1998 stands as the best American Olympic showing ever in this event.

In Nelson's view, the sport will always have limited appeal. "I don't think it's ever going to be a mass-appeal sport. What we have is a handful of really dedicated athletes who want to do it. Maybe we're working out of a group of 300 kids and we need to find the one who really wants to be an Olympian and understands about the commitment. But it's always been a small group."

According to Nelson, the typical biathlete comes from the ranks of skiers. "Usually it's the cross-country skier who's introduced to shooting. Most of them are skiers first that learn to shoot. It would be rather hard to be only a shooter and then try to develop the endurance and strength to become a quality cross-country skier without the appropriate physical background."

Other top American performers are the current world junior champion, Jay Hakkinen, and three-time Olympian Curtis Shreiner. Stacey Wooley has placed in the top ten in women's European races.

European athletes are expected to continue as masters of the biathlon. The Germans and Russians always field strong teams, and as Lyle Nelson adds, "any time you put skis on a Norwegian, they're going to be tough."

EQUIPMENT INSPECTION

To ensure that each competitor uses only approved equipment, officials inspect and mark all rifles and skis and determine that the athlete carries the correct amount of ammunition. The athlete must complete the course with those marked items. If a competitor arrives at the starting line without marked equipment, he or she is not permitted to start until the deficiency is corrected. The time required to do this is added to the overall time for the race.

BOBSLEDDING

One of winter sports' most exciting events is bobsledding. Teams of two or four athletes navigate a steep, twisting, icy course in specially designed sleds that reach speeds of up to 100 miles per hour. Bobsledding is especially popular in Europe and North America.

Origin of the Sport

Bobsledding originated in St. Moritz, Switzerland, in 1888 when a group of Americans and Englishmen came up with what they hoped would be an exciting improvement over tobogganing. They connected two sleds with a board and raced down the famous Cresta Run at St. Moritz at a much faster speed than a toboggan ever traveled. Ten years later the first organized competition took place in the same Swiss city with five-man teams. In 1902, St. Moritz became the home of the first specially built bobsled run. The sport received its name because early racers thought they could reach higher speeds by jerking their bodies backward and forward in a maneuver they called bobbing.

The first bobsled run in North America was built in 1911 near Quebec, Canada. The United States constructed its first bobsled run at Lake Placid, New York, in time for the 1932 Winter Olympics.

Competing in the Event

The riding surface of the steel, aluminum, or fiberglass sled, similar in shape to a bedroom slipper, measures about 11 feet (3.4 meters) in length for four-man teams and 9 ft (2.7 m) for two-man squads. The riding surface is attached to two supporting sleds with metal runners. The front sled swivels from side to side and is steered by means of a wheel or a rope, while the back sled supports the two- or four-man units. The back sled also contains the brake—a bar of hardened steel with serrated edges for cutting into ice. Total weight for bobsleds in the four-man event, including the crew, cannot exceed 1,389 pounds (630.6 kilograms). For the two-man event, the limit is 859 lbs (390 kg).

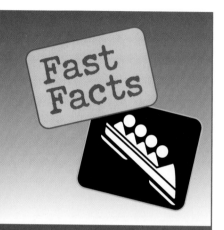

Fast Facts

First Olympic competition

Chamonix, France; 1924

Legendary athletes

William Fiske, USA

Wolfgang Hoppe,
East Germany

Eugenio Monti, Italy

Meinhard Nehmer,
East Germany

Criteria for winning

Fastest combined time of four runs

Athletes compete on a slippery course constructed by blanketing wet snow over a concrete or stone foundation and then soaking the snow with water to form ice. High banks of more snow and ice reach as high as 20 ft (6 m) in the turns, along both sides of the winding course. The banks help to keep the bobsled on course and protect spectators who line the route from serious injury should a sled career off the track. The risk of a sled flying off course is great, since the typical course contains as many as 26 tortuous turns along its 1,312- to 1,640-yard (1,200- to 1,500-meter) run.

At the start of the race, the team members take hold of the sled about 49 ft (15 m) behind the starting line and run forward, pushing the sled from behind or alongside to build up speed. As it approaches the starting line, the men jump into the sled and quickly duck down as it whisks along the course. When the sled enters the straightaways, the brakeman—who sits in the last spot, ready to halt the sled with the brake, orders the team to bob. In this maneuver, the members lean back in unison until they are practically lying flat on their backs, then snap

A four-man bobsled team pushes off at the start of a race. Bobsledders wear spiked shoes that enable them to grip the ice as they begin the course.

forward into a sitting position. This increases acceleration and helps the team reach the finish line more quickly.

The front man, called the driver, steers the bobsled. His responsibility is to execute the fastest possible run by properly negotiating the hairpin curves at speeds approaching 100 miles per hour. In four-man teams, the two athletes in the middle add weight to help control the sled. Also, by carefully shifting their weight from one side to the other, especially in the perilous turns, they help guide the sled down the run.

The winning team is the one that completes four separate runs in the lowest combined time. Over the life of the event, improved techniques and track conditions have dramatically lowered race times. Between 1932 and 1994, the winning time in the two-man event dropped from 8 minutes, 14.74 seconds, to less than 3.5 minutes. In 1984, WOLFGANG HOPPE of Germany set Olympic records in both the two-man event (3 minutes, 25.56 seconds) and four-man event (3 minutes, 20.22 seconds).

In the Olympics

In 1924, four-man bobsledding was added to the list of events at the Olympic Games in Chamonix, France. In the 1928 Winter Olympics in St. Moritz, Switzerland, the four-man event was switched to a five-man competition. When the Olympics moved to Lake Placid, New York, in 1932, the sport reverted to a four-man format, and a two-man event was added.

American teams dominated the first four Olympics that featured bobsledding, capturing 8 of 18 possible medals, including 2 gold medals in the two-man event and 2 in the four-man event. Until the mid-1950s, United States bobsledders led the way, mainly due to the efforts of Bob and Bill Linney, who had conceived a two-man sled with a steel plank as linkage in the late 1930s. The flexible steel link permitted greater speed in the turns. The Linney brothers also added side-mounted handles for better pushing and acceleration. In 1946 they developed the first all-steel sled, an innovation that greatly increased the sled's speed. These improvements helped United States bobsledders win at least one gold medal in each Olympics until 1952.

In the 1950s, teams from Switzerland and Germany, with financial backing from their governments, surpassed the Americans and have reigned supreme in the sport for much of the past 50 years. Meinhard Nehmer of Germany steered his bobsled to gold medals in the four-man event in 1976 and 1980 and added another gold in the two-man event in 1976. Wolfgang Hoppe, also of Germany, captured gold medals in both events in 1984. Swiss bobsled teams won gold medals in 1988 and 1992, while both Germany and Switzerland took gold medals in 1994. In the 1998 Winter Games, Germany's team took the gold medal in the four-man event with a time of 2 minutes, 39.41 seconds, while Canada's team swept to victory in the two-man competition with a time of 3 minutes, 37.24 seconds.

Numerous fascinating athletes appear in the pages of bobsledding history. Swiss competitor Felix Endrich exemplified both the joy and tragedy of competing in this danger-ous sport. In 1948, Endrich was half of the two-man Swiss team that sped to victory at St. Moritz in a time of 5 min-utes, 29.20 seconds. Five years later, one week after winning the world championship in the two-man bobsled, the 31-year-old Endrich died when his sled vaulted out of control over the bank and crashed into a tree.

The most renowned bob-sledder in the sport's history is Italian Eugenio Monti, who pi-loted 11 crews to world cham-pionships between 1957 and 1968. He experienced prob-lems capturing the Olympic gold, however. In the 1956 Win-ter Olympics in Cortina d'Am-pezzo, Italy, Monti missed gold medals in each event by slim margins.

To negotiate hairpin turns, bob-sled teams must shift their weight at precisely the right time.

SLEDDING IN JAMAICA

Despite the dangers and seriousness of the sport, Olympic bobsledding has had its lighter moments. In 1988 an American businessman sponsored a Jamaican team that included a helicopter pilot, a reggae singer, and a champion sprinter. Satisfying the eligibility requirements after only four months of training, the two-man team finished 35th, and the four-man team ended their run in a spectacular crash. Their story was featured in the 1993 movie *Cool Runnings*.

Good sportsmanship in the 1964 Winter Olympics at Innsbruck, Austria, may have cost Monti another gold medal. As the British team of Anthony Nash and Robin Dixon prepared for the two-man run, they noticed that a bolt had broken off their axle. They could not compete with this part missing. Little time remained before they had to head for the starting line when Monti came to their rescue. Standing nearby, he heard of their predicament, removed a bolt from his own sled, and sent it to his rivals. The British team attached the bolt and raced down the course to a gold medal.

Monti returned with a vengeance, however, in the 1968 games in Grenoble, France. He grabbed his first Olympic gold medal in the two-man event, registering a combined time of 4 minutes, 41.54 seconds, and followed it with a victory in the four-man event with a time of 2 minutes, 17.39 seconds. Monti ended his amazing Olympic career with two silver medals in 1956, two bronze medals in 1964, and two gold medals in 1968.

One of the most fascinating individuals in bobsled history is Billy Fiske of the United States. Fiske won two Olympic gold medals in the four-man event, the first in 1928 when he was only 16 years old. Four years later he ended up with a second gold medal in the same event in Lake Placid, New York.

Sadly, that was the final Olympic competition for the talented youth. When World War II erupted in Europe in 1939, Fiske was the first American to volunteer to fly for the besieged British Royal Air Force. Wounded during a flight over Germany in 1940, Fiske died before returning to the United States. In his honor, each year the Billy Fiske Memorial Trophy is awarded to the top American amateur bobsled team.

One man who raced with Fiske in 1932 made his own mark in sports history. Eddie Eagan had already won a gold medal in boxing in the 1920 Summer Olympics. With his medal in 1932 at Lake Placid, Eagan became the only American to win gold medals in both the Summer and Winter Olympics.

Since Eagan had never been on a bobsled before competing at Lake Placid, he signed a waiver absolving any American official of blame should he suffer an injury. His first ride in a bobsled had Eagan wondering if he had lost his sanity. He had lived through bloody encounters in the boxing ring, but nothing had prepared him for what he experienced. "The first ride will always be vivid in my memory," he explained later. "In a car, in the cab of a railroad engine, or in a plane, speed has never frightened me. But it did on that bobsled. It took only about two minutes to make that run, but to me it seemed like an eon. I remember the snow-covered ground flashing by like a motion picture out of focus. Speeding only a few inches from the ground without any sense of security, I hung on to the straps. My hands seemed to be slipping, but still I clung. We hit a turn. My head snapped backward. We went through Zigzag. I was dizzy as my head snapped first to the right, then to the left. Finally, the sled neared the bottom." A news reporter from the *New York Herald Tribune* who watched Eagan on his practice runs concluded that bobsledding was little more than a suicide attempt.

The 1980 games at Lake Placid, New York, saw the entry of the first African-Americans in the Winter Olympics. Willie Davenport, who had won a gold medal in the 110-meter high hurdle event in the 1968 Summer Games, teamed with Jeff Gadley and two other athletes to compete in the four-man bobsled event. The brave foursome finished a disappointing 12th.

Bobsledding is perilous enough without the extra dangers caused by poor weather. Warming temperatures, sleet, and poor visibility can transform a superbly maintained course into a deadly track. Athletes have often refused to compete until conditions improve. In the 1932 Olympics at Lake Placid, the four-man event had to be postponed until after the closing ceremony because of bad weather. Midway through the rescheduled run, the conditions worsened again, and many athletes walked off the course.

CURLING

Curling is an enormously popular sport in Canada. It is played on ice by two four-man teams that try to maneuver large stones toward targets. The name of the sport comes from the curling action that a player puts on the stone by twisting his wrist at delivery.

Origin of the Sport

Some controversy exists regarding the origin of curling. A 16th-century painting by Flemish artist Pieter Brueghel shows a scene of his countrymen playing a game that resembles curling. The Scots, however, reject the idea that the game started anywhere but in Scotland. As proof, Scots cite the fact that a curling stone dated 1551 was unearthed near Dunblane, Scotland, and that the people of Kilsyth, Scotland, started the first known curling organization in the 1500s.

What is indisputable is that the Scots refined and developed the game into what it is today. In 1838, standardized rules for the sport of curling were drawn up by John Cairnie and members of the Royal Caledonian Curling Club, which today regulates curling throughout the world. Cairnie was such an avid sportsman that he built the first artificial curling pond, called Curling Hall, at his home. Whenever the weather permitted, Cairnie raised a flag above his residence to signal that a game was about to begin.

In the early 1800s, Scottish soldiers stationed in Quebec, Canada, introduced curling to North America. In 1832, groups of athletes organized curling competitions in New England and northern Michigan.

Competing in the Event

The sheet of ice used in curling measures 138 feet long (42 meters) and just over 15 ft (4.6 m) wide—about one-sixth the size of a typical hockey rink. At each end of the sheet is the target, called a house, which consists of a tee surrounded by four concentric circles used in scoring. The crampit, a spiked metal plate from which the athletes deliver the stones, stands 3 to 4 yards (2.7–3.6 m) behind the house.

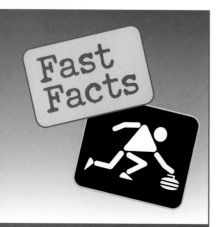

Fast Facts

First Olympic competition

Nagano, Japan; 1998

Legendary athletes

Glenn and Orvil Gilleshammer, USA

Raymond Somerville, USA

Criteria for winning

Highest score

A curling stone is one of the heaviest objects used in Olympic sports. It weighs 42.5 pounds (19 kilograms) and measures 36 inches (91.4 centimeters) in circumference. The stone has a handle on the portion that the competitors grasp for delivery. Most curling stones come from Scotland. These fine-grained stones retain little moisture as they glide across the ice, making it easy for curlers to control their path.

Team members use brooms to sweep the ice in front of the stone as it slides toward the house. Brooming melts the ice slightly and reduces the friction between the stone and the ice. As a result, the stone travels farther or veers from side to side. Skilled sweeping can add as much as 15 feet (4.6 m) to the distance a stone travels. The brooms have either short, fine bristles or longer, stiffer bristles. Brooms with fine bristles are used to push ice fragments in front of a stone to slow it down.

To deliver the stone, a player puts one foot on the crampit, takes hold of the handle, slides the stone back along the ice, and then gently releases it with a sliding, twisting motion. The twisting motion allows more control over the direction and speed of the stone. The team captain calls out directions to his teammates to tell them whether they should sweep the ice in front of the advancing stone to gain speed, permit the stone to deflect an opponent's stone farther from the tee, or try to stop the stone in a position that protects one of their earlier stones from being knocked away from the target.

Rules dictate that teams follow a set order in delivering the stones. The least experienced member of the team usually goes first,

Mike Peplinski, a member of the American Olympic curling team, prepares to slide a stone across the ice.

ALL IN THE FAMILY

The best American curler, RAYMOND "BUD" SOMERVILLE, came by his skill naturally. His father, a national curling champion, taught him the game when Bud was a youngster. Somerville became the first American to win a world championship, a victory that helped earn him a place in the United States Curling Hall of Fame.

Now retired from competitive curling, Somerville enjoys watching his son, Tim, curl. Like his own father, Somerville has passed on his skills to Tim, who has made a name for himself in American curling.

because he or she will not have to worry about other stones on the ice. Then come the number two and number three players, with the captain sliding the final stone.

Each player slides two stones from the crampit toward the house at the opposite end of the rink. Competitors deliver one stone at a time, alternating with their opponents. The players complete an end, or inning, when all 16 stones have been delivered. The teams then move to the opposite end of the rink for the next inning. A typical curling game, called a bonspiel, lasts ten ends, although the team captains may agree beforehand to a shorter or longer match.

Strategy is very important in curling. Team members look not only at stopping a stone close to the tee but also at positioning the first seven stones so that the eighth one knocks them closer to the tee or deflects the opponent's stones out of the circle. Proximity to the tee determines how many points a team receives each inning. Each stone that is closer to the tee than the closest stone of the other team receives a point. Only one team can score points, with an eight-point maximum for each end. A measuring instrument is used to determine which stone is closest to the tee.

In the Olympics

Curling was included as a demonstration sport in four different Olympics: 1924, 1932, 1988, and 1992. In that last appearance as a demonstration sport, the best-known American curler, Raymond "Bud" Somerville, helped his team win a bronze medal.

A few months after the 1992 games in Albertville, France, the International Olympic Committee approved curling as a medal sport starting with the 1998 games in Nagano, Japan. Canadian athletes lived up to expectations by taking the gold medal in the women's event and a silver in the men's competition. The Swiss team walked away with the gold medal in the men's event.

FIGURE SKATING

Figure skating is similar to ballet dancing on ice—a sport in which athletes jump, twirl, or dance to music. Competitors are judged according to the difficulty and gracefulness of their moves. Although figure skating has been popular for decades, it has enjoyed immense growth in recent years.

THE HISTORY OF SKATING

Although no one can determine the exact date of origin of the sport of ice-skating, evidence that skates existed as far back as 50 B.C. was found in ancient Roman ruins in London. Among the discoveries were leather soles and blades fashioned from polished animal bones. Finns and Laplanders, who slid across the snow on snowshoes and runners, were called "Sliding Finns" in ancient Norwegian sagas, and children's literature frequently mentioned the Dutch skating on their numerous canals.

Metal blades were first used in the 1500s and even played a major role in determining the outcome of a war. In 1572, Dutch soldiers wore skates in their battle to rescue Amsterdam from invading Spanish troops. Their extraordinary mobility on the ice saved the day.

Origin of the Sport

The world's first skating club was organized in Scotland in 1642. When Scottish and other European settlers arrived in the New World, they brought the sport with them. Ice-skating became very popular in the northern United States and in Canada, where longer, colder winters provided ideal conditions for skating. Philadelphians organized the first American skating club in 1849.

The switch to steel blades reduced the friction and made it possible for skaters to experiment with spins and jumps. American skater and ballet teacher Jackson Haines revolutionized ice-skating by combining skating and dancing. He introduced grace and fluidity to a sport that had become somewhat rigid. His innovations stirred hostility among traditionalists in the

Fast Facts

First Olympic competition

London, Great Britain; 1908

Legendary athletes

Tenley Albright, USA

Richard Button, USA

Peggy Fleming, USA

Ekaterina Gordeeva and Sergei Grinkov, Soviet Union

Sonja Henie, Norway

Jayne Torvill and Christopher Dean, Great Britain

Katarina Witt, East Germany

Criteria for winning

Highest score

United States who insisted that the sport not be altered. Haines encountered less opposition in Europe, where audiences praised his creativity.

Three other skaters were instrumental in changing figure skating in North America. In the 1880s, Louis Rubenstein of Montreal, Canada, helped shape the Canadian Figure Skating Association and the United States Figure Skating Association. His disciples, George H. Browne and Irving Brokaw of Cambridge, Massachusetts, spread Rubenstein's ideas by demonstrating his format for competitions. In 1914, Browne organized the first International Figure Skating Championships of America to promote Rubenstein's ideas and boost the reputation of the United States among other figure-skating nations. Browne's work led to the 1921 formation of the United States Figure Skating Association to govern and promote the sport.

The introduction of artificial ice boosted figure skating by enabling athletes to practice their sport year-round on indoor skating rinks. The first rink opened in London, England, in 1876; an American rink followed in New York City three years later.

Before the early 1920s, any skater who felt qualified could enter a competition. Since that time, however, skaters have had to exhibit their mastery of figure skating in a series of tests before becoming eligible to participate in competitive events. Formal ice-dancing tests appeared in 1938, and tests for pairs were initiated in the 1950s.

In 1896, Russia hosted the first men's World Championship figure skating competition. Ten years later a similar event was held for women. Figure skating was added to the Olympics held in London, England, in 1908. The popularity of figure skating helped inspire a festival of winter sports.

The first figure skater to gain international recognition was Norwegian SONJA HENIE, who skyrocketed to fame by winning Norway's championship at age ten. Henie held the world title for ten consecutive years in the 1920s and 1930s and captured Olympic gold medals in 1928, 1932, and 1936.

The first American to capture the national title was DICK BUTTON. He won the title in 1946 at age 16 and remained a champion for the next six years. Button won Olympic gold medals in 1948 and 1952, during a time in which he was the reigning world champion for five straight years.

Figure skating has seen many other talented champions, including Scott Hamilton, Dorothy Hamill, and Peggy Fleming of the United States, and KATARINA WITT of East Germany. Great Britain's ice dancing team of JAYNE TORVILL AND CHRISTOPHER DEAN popularized that event throughout the world with their sensual, graceful performances. Between 1975 and 1995, the couple won more than 20 national and international competitions.

Competing in the Event

Equipment for figure skating includes skating boots and blades, a costume, and music. The boots are made from leather or other durable material and have high tops to support the skater's ankles. The boots rest on a blade one-eighth inch thick and about 1 foot long. Depending on which spin or leap the skater makes, the blade's inside and outside edges carry the weight of the skater as he or she lands on the surface of the ice. Several teeth, called toe picks, at the front of the blade enable skaters to dig into the ice as they begin a leap.

Figure skaters' costumes combine elegance and comfort while allowing free movement around the ice. Women athletes usually wear short skirts with tights, while men wear close-fitting full-length trousers and a top. Athletes may select their own outfits, but they must be modest and dignified in the opinion of the Olympic judges.

Figure skating rinks are approximately 200 feet (61 meters) long and 80 ft (24 m) wide. A barrier about 4 ft (1.2 m) high, with gently rounded corners, surrounds the rink. Olympic skating arenas are built to hold at least 15,000 spectators.

Figure skaters compete in men's and women's singles and as couples in the pairs and ice dancing competitions. Athletes select their own musical accompaniment. The only requirement is that the music not contain vocal sections. Music helps communicate the character of the routine.

Singles skating consists of the short skating program followed by the free-skating program. The short program, which accounts for one-third of the skater's total score, requires that each skater execute the same three jumps, three spins, and fast-step sequences or combinations. The routine must be completed within 2 minutes and 40 seconds. Judges evaluate figure skaters on a point basis ranging from 0 to 6, with 6 being a perfect score. When judges watch a performance, they look for more than grace. The position of the body and arms during various moves are crucial to a good score, as is the difficulty of each maneuver. Judges award points in two areas: technical merit, which measures precision of movement; and artistic impression, which scores the skater's artistry, choreography, and style.

The free-skating program gives more freedom to the skater, but it still must be meticulously choreographed. The 4-minute women's and 4½-minute men's program are typically filled with more daring leaps and jumps, flashier costumes, and originality of style that is lacking in the short program. Since the scores count for two-thirds of the total score, figure skaters save their best and most difficult moves for this part of the competition. Judges award points in a fashion similar to the short program, but they also look for creativity, versatility, and innovation in the moves. In the event of a tie, the winner is the skater who received the highest scores in the long or free-skating program.

Before 1990, skaters also had to compete in the compulsory figures. Compulsories required the athletes to make a figure eight in the ice with their blades, then repeatedly skate over the figure eight without going outside the curves. Although this repetitive form of skating displayed the skaters' precision and discipline, it never caught on with the spectators or television audiences. Due to a lack of popularity, officials finally dropped the compulsories.

In pairs skating, a male and female skater perform a series of moves as a couple. Exact timing and synchronization of movements are critical to winning. Even

American figure skater Kristi Yamaguchi spins on the ice during the women's singles competition at the 1992 games. Yamaguchi won the gold medal in this event.

when the skaters are apart, their movements must mirror each other's. Some of skating's most spectacular moments happen in pairs competition. The sport blends athleticism and daring spins with a romantic element created by the two skaters as they coordinate their moves so closely.

The pairs competition also has a short program counting for one-third of their score and a free-skating program counting for two-thirds. The short program lasts 2 minutes and 40 seconds and requires each pair to execute eight moves, including overhead lifts, side-by-side solo jumps, solo spins, and intricate footwork.

The free-skating program lasts 4 minutes and 30 seconds. Spectators love watching this exciting part of the competition, which blends athletic skill, agility, and romance. Couples are allowed more freedom to choose their moves and skate to their strengths. They glide across the ice, lift off in matching jumps, and hold each other in high-speed spins. Double and triple jumps, in which the skaters twirl in the air two or three times before returning to the ice, are sprinkled between shadow skating and mirror skating. In shadow skating, the pairs perform identical moves while apart; in mirror skating, they skate in opposite directions and mirror each other's moves.

Whereas individual and pairs skating are reminiscent of ballet, ice dancing resembles ballroom dancing because it focuses on the various forms of dance rather than on jumps and spins. Rhythm, interpretation of music, and precision of movement are important features of the sport. Except for brief moments, ice dancers must remain in contact with each other during the entire program.

The ice dancing program consists of three parts. Two compulsory dances, worth 20 percent of the final score, require all pairs to perform the same dances, such as the waltz, tango, or jitterbug. Each couple must properly execute all the moves demanded by those dances. In the original dance, counting for 30 percent of the score, couples dance to the same rhythm and tempo but create original dance moves to their own music. Judges evaluate the skaters on originality and interpretation of music.

The free dance counts for 50 percent of the total score and is therefore extremely important. Skaters have 4 minutes to

JUDGING THE COMPETITION

Olympic judges use the following scale to evaluate performances in all figure skating competitions:

Points	Meaning
0	did not skate
1	bad, very poor
2	poor
3	average
4	good
5	excellent
6	perfect

Judges may use numbers between those shown above to indicate a performance falling somewhere between the whole numbers. For instance, a judge might award a 5.6 for a performance that was excellent but not perfect.

exhibit their technical skills and creativity in their choice of program and choreography. Judges rate skaters on their originality, timing, precision, and teamwork.

In the Olympics

Before the first Winter Olympics in 1924, figure skating was an event in the Summer Games. Madge Syers of Great Britain won the women's individual gold medal in 1908 in London, England, and pairs skaters Anna Hübler and Heinrich Burger of Germany took the gold. Ulrich Salchow of Sweden grabbed most of the attention, however, when he introduced a jump—now called the Salchow—during his gold medal performance in the men's individual competition. The Salchow requires a skater to take off from the back inside edge of one skate, execute one complete turn in the air, and land on the back outside edge of the opposite skate. It was the first in a series of innovations brought to the sport by daring and imaginative athletes.

Sweden produced the first Olympic figure skating star. Beginning with the 1920 Olympics in Antwerp, Belgium, Gillis Grafström dominated the men's individual event by capturing three straight gold medals. He defeated Norway's Andreas Krogh and bested Austria's Willy Böckl at both Chamonix, France, in 1924 and St. Moritz, Switzerland, in 1928. He triumphed in 1928 in spite of a painful knee injury.

With the growing popularity of skating and skiing, Olympic officials decided in 1924 to organize a separate Winter Olympics. Herma Planck-Szabo of Austria won the women's individual figure skating competition, but these games were noteworthy because of the first Olympic appearance of 11-year-old Sonja Henie. Though the Norwegian athlete finished in eighth place, she was on her way to a remarkable career of Olympic triumphs.

A combination of elegance, athleticism, and beauty brought Henie gold medals in 1928, 1932, and 1936. Unlike competitors before her, and matched by few after her, Henie attempted to tell a story with her balletic moves. In addition to her Olympic success, she won ten consecutive World Championships before she retired in 1936. Almost single-handedly,

Henie popularized figure skating around the world, first as a competitive performer and then as a movie star. Between 1938 and 1960, the Norwegian athlete showcased her remarkable skating talents in 11 feature films. By the time she died in 1969, she had amassed a fortune estimated at almost $50 million.

Figure skating was held indoors for the first time during the 1932 Games at Lake Placid, New York. While Henie continued her domination of the women's side of the sport, Gillis Grafström's reign ended when the three-time defending gold medalist lost an exciting contest to Karl Schäfer of Austria. By taking the silver medal, Grafström became the first athlete to win medals in four different Winter Olympics.

Two German skaters, 30-year-old Ernst Baier and 15-year-old Maxi Herber, made history in the 1936 games by introducing what has become a staple of pairs competition: shadow skating. The couple, who later married, had to execute a series of identical moves without touching each other. Their innovative approach won them the gold medal.

Following a 12-year hiatus imposed by World War II, the games resumed in 1948 in St. Moritz, Switzerland. A Harvard freshman from the United States, DICK BUTTON, won the first of two successive gold medals in the men's individual by including the difficult double axel in his program. This move requires the athlete to glide forward on one foot, leap from the outside edge of the forward skate, rotate two and a half times in the air, and land on the opposite skate while skating backward. Never before performed in figure skating, Button had landed the move successfully only once in practice—and that was only two days before the Olympic event. In spite of some doubts whether he would include the move in his program, which would cost him the championship if he faltered, Button executed the double axel successfully.

Button later said that his gamble offered a challenge he felt compelled to accept: "The thing I remember most, the moment that mattered, was the day before the Olympics when I went through a clean double axel. No one else in the world had done one and I had worked it into my routine. That is what you remember. That is what has meaning."

While Sonja Henie incorporated elegance and ballet moves into her skating, Button chose a vigorous approach that focused on high jumps and athletic steps. The sport has greatly benefited from the double dose of grace and athleticism that these two gifted skaters brought to their performances.

Barbara Ann Scott of Canada had reason to both curse and celebrate the events of the 1948 games at St. Moritz. One year before the Olympics, her hometown of Ottawa, Canada, wanted to present her with a canary yellow convertible automobile in recognition of her astounding successes. The head of the International Olympic Committee, Avery Brundage, learned of the plan and threatened to ban Scott from the 1948 Olympic Games unless she declined the expensive gift. If she accepted the car, he said, Scott would relinquish her amateur standing and thus be ineligible to compete.

Scott, whose focus was set on Olympic gold, had little choice but to turn down the car. Other female skaters may have wished that Brundage had allowed her to keep it, because Scott skated with a vengeance at St. Moritz. Her gold medal performance lifted her above Austria's Eva Pawlik and Great Britain's Jeanette Altwegg. In the end, Scott received the best of everything. Three months after winning at the Olympics, she turned professional and accepted Ottawa's gift.

In Oslo, Norway, four years later, the American skating team exhibited one of its strongest showings in Olympic history when every member of the figure skating team placed in the top five. American men grabbed three of the top four spots, including a gold and a bronze, while the women took second, fourth, and fifth spots. Dick Button led the medals parade by capturing his second consecutive gold medal. He followed his 1948 introduction of the double axel by successfully including another new move—the triple loop. This move required Button to take off from the edge of one blade, make three complete revolutions in the air, and land on the same foot and edge.

Button almost stumbled because the surface of the ice was choppy. In typical fashion, he blamed the near-mishap on himself. "The ice is never bad," Button explained, "only the skater is."

American skaters registered another impressive showing in the 1956 games at Cortina d'Ampezzo, Italy, when they took all three medal spots in the men's competition and the top two medals in the women's event. Hayes Alan Jenkins, who had missed a bronze medal in 1952 by a slim margin, finally reaped the benefits of his rigorous training regimen by winning the gold medal. For almost a decade, the young athlete had practiced 40 hours a week, 10 months a year preparing for the Olympics. The United States completed a sweep when Ronald Robertson and Hayes's younger brother, David Jenkins, won silver and bronze medals respectively. Not since 1908 had one nation claimed all three medal spots in men's competition.

American skater TENLEY ALBRIGHT displayed courage and determination in winning the women's competition. Stricken with polio at the age of 11, Albright overcame her illness and steadily advanced in the world of figure skating. After winning a silver medal in 1952, Albright was the favorite to take home the top spot at Cortina d'Ampezzo. But, just two weeks before the games, Albright badly injured her right foot in practice when her skate hit a rut in the ice. As she fell, her left skate blade slashed the boot of her right foot and cut a vein. Her father, a surgeon, attended to her injury, and Albright went on to win the gold medal.

The United States was not so fortunate in the pairs competition, where the team of Carole Ormaca and Robin Greiner placed fifth. This event, though, is best remembered for its controversial outcome. The crowd had been pulling for a young German couple to win a medal, and their victory seemed assured when Frances Dafoe of the Canadian pairs lost her balance during her performance. The judges refused to substantially penalize the Canadian couple, however, and when the marks were posted, Dafoe and her partner placed second and the German pair placed fourth. The unhappy crowd erupted in catcalls and jeers and began tossing oranges onto the ice and at the judges.

Russian figure skater Anton Sikharulidze holds up partner Elena Berezhnaya during a skating exhibition at the 1998 Winter Olympics. They won the silver medal in the pairs competition.

AIR TRAGEDY

When an airliner crashed at Berg, near Brussels, Belgium, on February 15, 1961, it took more than the lives of American athletes. It shattered the Owens family. Maribel Vinson Owens, who had won a bronze medal in the 1932 Olympic Games, was accompanying the United States team to Europe where her two daughters, Laurence and Maribel, were to compete. All three perished in the crash, which also took the lives of five skaters who had participated in the 1960 games at Squaw Valley, California.

The amazing run by American skaters continued in 1960 at Squaw Valley, California. David Jenkins, who described his performance as one of his best, succeeded his brother as the gold medalist in the men's event. In women's skating, Carol Heiss won the gold medal and Barbara Roles earned a bronze. In pairs competition, the American team of Nancy and Ronald Ludington added another bronze medal.

Heiss had extra incentive to skate her best. Shortly before the games started, Heiss's mother died from cancer. Heiss vowed to win the gold medal in her honor. Her motivation earned her the first place votes of all nine judges.

A report from the United States Olympic Committee describes Heiss's performance as a "magnificent exhibition in the free skating that stirred a capacity crowd of 8,500 to tears and cheers. Clad in a crimson costume, embellished with spangles and a tiara in her blonde hair, she bedazzled the judges, her opposition, and the spectators with her sheer artistry."

With its recent domination in figure skating—and talented younger skaters waiting in the wings—the United States team looked forward to years of medal-winning exhibitions. This abruptly ended on February 15, 1961, when the airplane carrying the United States team to the world championships in Prague, Czechoslovakia, crashed in Belgium. All 73 people aboard were killed, including 18 team members, 5 coaches, and numerous friends and relatives.

The results three years later in Innsbruck, Austria, were predictable for the new United States team. Fourteen-year-old Scott Allen won a silver medal, the only award for the United States team in men's competition. This was the beginning of the rise of the Soviet Union in the figure-skating world. The dynamic pair of Ludmilla Belousova and Oleg Protopopov led their opponents with a breathtaking exhibition. The couple, who later married, skated with a passion no others could match. They also introduced the spectacular death spiral, a move in which Protopopov spun in a pivot position while holding the hand of Belousova, who swirled on one skate as she lowered her body parallel and close to the ice. Bold and daring, the move has since become a fixture in pairs competition.

One sports magazine described the Soviet pair's performance in glowing terms: "The graceful, calculated movements of the Protopopovs made their difficult overhead lifts look deceptively simple. Their best-remembered gimmick always will be Ludmilla's daring ability to caress the ice with her blonde hair during their smoothly slow death spirals, with even her waist swinging only inches above the frozen surface."

As expected, at the 1968 games in Grenoble, France, the Protopopovs won a second gold medal. Oleg Protopopov later explained the secret of their success to the press: "Art cannot be measured by points. We skate from the heart. To us it is spiritual beauty that matters." He added that the growing popularity of brother-sister pairs skaters perplexed him. "These pairs of brother and sister, how can they convey the emotion, the love, that exists between a man and a woman? That is what we try to show."

The newest star in the individual competition came once again from the United States. After placing sixth at the games in Innsbruck in 1964, Peggy Fleming went on to earn a gold medal at the games in 1968. Wearing beautiful, flowing outfits designed and sewn by her mother, Fleming took the only U.S. gold medal in the Olympics.

Ondrej Nepela from Czechoslovakia edged out Sergei Tchetveroukhin of the Soviet Union to win the 1972 gold medal in the men's singles figure skating at Sapporo, Japan. Austrian Beatrix Schuba defeated two North American skaters, Karen Magnussen of Canada and Janet Lynn of the United States, in the women's competition. A new Soviet star in pairs skating, Irina Rodnina, won her first of three straight gold medals with partner Alexei Ulanov. Rodnina repeated her win in the 1976 Olympic Games, once again at Innsbruck, Austria, this time with a new partner—Alexander Saizev.

Bigger news came from the 1976 men's singles competition when American skater Tony Kubicka made headlines by including a backflip in his program. Olympic officials later declared the move too dangerous and banned it from future competitions.

John Curry of Great Britain won the 1976 men's gold, and Dorothy Hamill from the United States took the women's gold. The superstitious Hamill, who wore a four-leaf clover on the left shoulder of her costume because it was Friday the 13th, skated a beautiful program to take top honors. "I was so keyed up I never wanted to go to bed," the victorious Hamill said afterward. When she finally did go to sleep, she had her gold medal safely tucked under her pillow.

Ice dancing was introduced as a competitive event in the 1976 games. Two pairs of Soviet skaters took the gold and silver medals, while an American couple was awarded the bronze medal. Ice dancing has since become one of the most popular events in the Winter Olympics.

American skaters Tai Babilonia and Randy Gardner were expected to offer a challenge for the gold medal in pairs skating at the 1980 games in Lake Placid, New York. Shortly before the competition, however, Gardner suffered a severe groin injury when he fell four times during the warm-ups. As a result, the couple had to withdraw from competition. The happiest skater, no doubt, was Irina Rodnina, who won her third consecutive gold medal. In addition to her three gold medals, Rodnina had skated to ten World Championships, placing her in the same league as the legendary Sonja Henie.

Russian skaters Oksana Grishuk and Yevgeny Platov dance across the ice at the 1998 games.

The 1984 Olympics in Sarajevo, Yugoslavia, introduced several new skating stars to the sport. Jayne Torvill and Christopher Dean of Great Britain electrified audiences with their creative ice-dancing programs. Their skill and inventiveness led to a perfect score and an Olympic gold medal. In the women's individual competition, Katarina Witt of East Germany took top honors, winning her first of two gold medals. Popular men's skater Scott Hamilton of the United States won the gold medal in the men's individual event.

Two Brians, Boitano of the United States and Orser of Canada, staged a thrilling competition in front of Orser's home crowd in Calgary, Canada, in 1988. Orser lost points when he stumbled slightly in his long program, and the gold went to Boitano. Debra Thomas of the United States made history by becoming the first African-American athlete to win a medal in the Winter Olympics. Her bronze medal placed her behind Canada's Elizabeth Manley and East Germany's Katarina Witt.

In pairs skating, the Soviet Union's EKATERINA GORDEEVA AND SERGEI GRINKOV skated to a first-place finish by including what became their trademark quadruple twist lift. The married couple brought a passion to their skating that was reminiscent of their predecessors, Ludmilla Belousova and Oleg Protopopov.

The 1994 Olympic Games at Lillehammer, Norway, were charged with emotion. After a six-year absence to have a child and skate professionally, Gordeeva and Grinkov took advantage of a new rule that allowed professionals to re-apply for amateur status. The couple showed the same daring form that had brought them awards and praise earlier, and earned yet another gold medal. In the men's competition, Elvis Stojko of Canada showed an energetic style, which won over the audiences, though some of the more conservative judges were not impressed. Stojko's high jumps and spectacular spins were breathtaking. Fellow athletes Alexei Urmanov of Russia and Philippe Candeloro of France also skated daring, electrifying programs. The trio represented a new wave in men's figure skating.

The biggest story from the 1994 Olympics involved two American skaters, Nancy Kerrigan and Tonya Harding. Kerrigan had been assaulted after a practice session for the

National Championship in Boston. The resulting knee injury forced her to pull out of the competition, but she was back in form ready for the Olympics. When Harding's ex-husband confessed to the assault, suspicion emerged about Tonya Harding's role in the sordid affair.

A circus atmosphere surrounded the women's individual event, as reporters tried to pry inflammatory comments from Kerrigan and Harding. The nervous Harding skated poorly and finished in 10th place, while Kerrigan took a silver medal behind the Ukraine's Oksana Baiul. Subsequent findings in the assault investigation led the United States Figure Skating Association to ban Harding from the sport for life.

In the 1998 games at Nagano, Japan, United States skater Todd Eldridge, four-time national champion and the favorite, failed to win an Olympic medal. Six years earlier at Albertville he had placed a distant 10th after experiencing back problems and had failed to make the team in 1994. Declaring 1998 as his last opportunity for a medal, Eldridge skated one of the best programs of his career, but just missed the bronze medal. In the women's event, Tara Lipinski of the United States captured the gold medal. At age 15, she was the youngest gold medalist in figure skating history.

FREESTYLE SKIING

A newcomer to Olympic sports, freestyle skiing combines parts of the downhill race with spins and twists often found in snowboarding. Enthusiasts in both freestyle skiing and snowboarding attempt moves not seen in Alpine or Nordic skiing.

◀ SEE HISTORY OF SKIING ON PAGE 18.

Origin of the Sport

Americans popularized freestyle skiing in the 1960s and 1970s as a demonstration event. Since no rigid set of rules stood in their way, only the athlete's own sense of caution and lack of inspiration held them back from coming up with more and more creative stunts. From the California ski slopes and the hills of New England, daredevil athletes tried to outdo one another. Freestyle skiing was shunned by the establishment at first because it was considered too radical a departure from Alpine and Nordic skiing. A variety of injuries associated with the new sport also came under scrutiny.

Still, spectators flocked to freestyle skiing tournaments because they appreciated the athleticism of the competitors and loved the breathtaking maneuvers. In 1979, the International Ski Federation finally recognized the sport and established a World Cup circuit in freestyle skiing. Since the beginning, the World Cup competition has been dominated by American skiers.

Competing in the Event

Olympic freestyle skiing consists of two separate competitions—the moguls and the aerials. In moguls, or bump freestyle skiing, athletes race down a steep slope covered with numerous small mounds while performing jumps and other acrobatic moves to their choice of music.

Competition usually consists of two rounds. Seven judges evaluate the athletes for their speed, execution of turns, the creativity of their program, and their ability to handle the bumps gracefully. After the highest and lowest marks are thrown out, the top 16 skiers advance to the final round. The

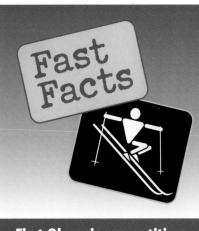

Fast Facts

First Olympic competition

Albertville, France; 1992

Legendary athletes

Jean-Luc Brassard, **Canada**

Jonny Moseley, **USA**

Andreas Schoenbaechler, **Switzerland**

Nikki Stone, **USA**

Criteria for winning

Highest score

A freestyle skier executes a spread-eagle maneuver during the moguls competition at the 1994 games.

best performer in the second round wins the gold medal.

Athletes can select any music they wish. Unlike other Olympic competitions involving music, such as figure skating and ice dancing, where romantic ballads or classical melodies can often be heard, in the moguls the preferred sounds are rock and rap.

While the moguls competition is a unique format of downhill skiing, the aerials require more daring maneuvers. Some observers have called this type of skiing "diving on skis" because the athletes ski down a hill, leap from a raised platform, and go through a series of twists, flips, and spins before landing. The performer must execute a series of acrobatic moves while soaring as high as 60 feet (18 meters) in the air.

Judges look for creativity and daring, difficulty of moves, and skill of execution, including the landing. Technique and form count for 50 percent of the final score; proper takeoff and height count for 20 percent; and a successful landing counts for the final 30 percent.

In the Olympics

Freestyle skiing was first seen as a demonstration sport in the 1988 Winter Games at Calgary, Canada. Four years later, the sport achieved medal status when mogul events for men and women were included at the games in Albertville, France. Donna Weinbrecht of the United States, a two-time World Cup champion and the heavy favorite to win at Albertville, took the women's gold medal, while Edgar Grospiron of France delighted his countrymen by winning the men's gold.

The medal did not come easily to Weinbrecht, even though she had won eight World Cup races in 1990, seven in 1991, and eight more in 1992 before heading into the Olympics. She concentrated so intensely on doing well in the games that she became ill from the stress. Putting health concerns aside, though, she put on a clutch performance.

Aerial freestyle made its first appearance at the games in Lillehammer, Norway, two years later. Andreas Schoenbaechler of Switzerland and Lina Cherjazava of Uzbekistan captured gold medals in the men's and women's aerials respectively. The 1992 bronze medalist in the moguls, Stine Lise Hattestad of Norway, skiing before a receptive crowd of fellow Norwegians who lined the course, edged out Liz McIntyre from the United States for the women's gold medal, while Jean-Luc Brassard of Canada took the men's gold.

The intense Brassard, born in Quebec, rode to success not for his speed but for the superb technique and the extra height he seemed to pull out of each jump. Brassard had the ability to combine athleticism with a natural sense of showmanship. One of his coaches once remarked, "You've got to have a bit of flair for the dramatic to excel in this sport. And Jean-Luc definitely has that."

Olympians from the United States put on a show for spectators at Nagano, Japan, in 1998 by taking three of the four gold medals in freestyle skiing. Jonny Moseley of Tiburon, California, grabbed first place in the men's moguls, while Eric Bergoust added a gold medal in the men's aerials.

The United States split the gold medals in women's events, winning the top spot in the aerials when Nikki Stone, a four-time United States champion and gymnastics devotee, defeated Xu Nannan of China and Colette Brand of Switzerland. But the biggest thrill for the host country came when Japan's Tae Satoya took the gold in women's moguls. The spectators went wild.

A CROWD PLEASER

Like snowboarding, freestyle skiing faced strong opposition at first. Purists claimed that the participants in the new events were little more than reckless amateurs trying to shock people with their death-defying stunts. The term *hotdogging* appeared in many newspaper and magazine articles to describe freestyle skiing. Critics also pointed to the alarming number of injuries that plagued the sport.

Spectators, however, flocked to freestyle events. They loved to watch the moguls and aerials and came in large numbers whenever a competition was staged. By the 1980s, a World Cup had been organized, and freestyle skiing had joined the community of worldwide sports.

ICE HOCKEY

Ice hockey is a fast-moving sport played by two teams of six players. The teams attempt to shoot a hard rubber disk, called a puck, past the opposing goalie into the net. Immensely popular in Canada, the game also has a strong following in the United States and northern European countries.

Origin of the Sport

The exact origin of ice hockey may never be known. The sport probably began in Great Britain or France more than 500 years ago. In fact, the sport probably received its name from the French word *hoquet,* which means "bent stick." The French loved to play field hockey in the summer and then switch to a similar game on frozen ponds and streams in the winter. The Dutch engaged in a sport called *kolven* in the 1600s, and Englishmen popularized a game called bandy, in which athletes skated on frozen fields, hitting a wooden or cork ball with wooden sticks.

Hockey was introduced to the New World by British soldiers, who played a version of the sport on frozen ponds in Nova Scotia. In 1855, soldiers from the Royal Canadian Rifles organized an informal league of teams near Kingston, Ontario, and the game of hockey as we know it today was born.

Within 20 years, college students began playing hockey at McGill University in Montreal. W. F. Robertson, a student at the university, adapted the rules of field hockey for the ice. An amateur league arose in the Kingston area in 1885, and Canadian governor general Lord Stanley of Preston offered a trophy to the best Canadian team in 1893. Winning that trophy, known as the Stanley Cup, became the main objective of serious hockey clubs in Canada. Professional hockey clubs began to emerge after 1908, and today the Stanley Cup is given to the championship team of the National Hockey League.

The first professional hockey league appeared in the United States in 1904. Called the International Pro Hockey League, it operated in the upper peninsula of Michigan. When it folded three years later, the National Hockey Association took its place. In 1908, the International Ice Hockey Federation was born to regulate the sport.

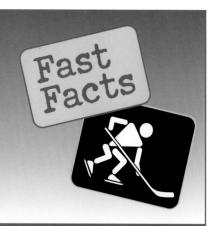

Fast Facts

First Olympic competition

Men's:
Antwerp, Belgium; 1920

Women's:
Nagano, Japan; 1998

Legendary athletes

James Craig, **USA**

Mike Eruzione, **USA**

Vladislav Tretiak, **Soviet Union**

Criteria for winning

Highest score

The National Hockey League, formed in 1917, consisted of five teams—two from Montreal and one each from Toronto, Ottawa, and Quebec—that played a 22-game season. Seven years later, the Boston Bruins became the first United States team to join the league. Soon teams from New York, Chicago, and Detroit also entered competition.

For much of its early history, the league was made up of what are now referred to as the "original six" teams: Montreal Canadiens, Toronto Maple Leafs, Boston Bruins, New York Rangers, Chicago Black Hawks, and Detroit Red Wings. In the 1990s, the league grew to more than 20 teams.

In the 1950s, two teams dominated play in the National Hockey League. From the 1949–1950 season through the 1959–1960 season, Gordie Howe's Detroit Red Wings and Maurice "Rocket" Richard's Montreal Canadiens captured nine of ten Stanley Cups. Although there have been some powerhouse teams since then, league play has been more balanced.

In addition to Howe and Richard, other players have had a big impact on professional hockey. As a member of the Boston Bruins, Bobby Orr transformed the defensive position with his ability to score and handle the puck. Wayne Gretzky broke almost every scoring record imaginable in his illustrious career with the Edmonton Oilers and several other teams.

Dominated for years by Canada, hockey changed dramatically in 1972 with the first series of games between the stars of Canada and the powerful Soviet Union team. While everyone expected the Canadians to crush their foe, the Soviets skated with finesse and speed and passed the puck with pinpoint accuracy to keep pace with the favored Canadians. Although they lost the deciding game, the Soviet team announced that Canada no longer owned hockey.

Twelve nations are eligible to participate in hockey at the Winter Games. The top ten teams based on the previous year's world championships join the defending Olympic champion and a team from the host nation. The 12 teams are organized into two groups, with each group participating in a round-robin series of five games. The top two teams in each division move on to the semifinals and play for the gold medal.

MEN ON ICE

In the early days of ice hockey, there were nine men on the ice. The number dropped to seven in the late 1880s after a club participating in the Montreal Winter Carnival arrived two men short. Showing excellent sportsmanship, the opposing team agreed to play with only seven men, and over a period of time athletes found the smaller number of players on ice offered more freedom and maneuverability, and brought greater excitement to the game. When the National Hockey League was established in 1917, it dropped the seventh player and standardized the number of players to six. That number has remained constant ever since.

Although women's hockey had been played as far back as 1892, the first world championship was not organized until 1990. The sport has since gained in popularity, and it is now one of the Winter Olympics competitions. Women played for Olympic medals in hockey for the first time in 1998, when the United States defeated Canada in the gold medal match.

Competing in the Event

A hockey rink measures 100 feet (30.5 meters) wide by 200 feet (61 m) long. A solid wall of white wood or fiberglass, topped with a 4-ft (1.2-m) section of safety glass, encloses the rink to protect the spectators.

Colored lines divide the ice into zones. A red line cuts the rink into two halves. Red goal lines run across the ice 10 ft (3 m) from the end of the rink. In the middle of these lines stand the goal cages, 4 ft (1.2 m) high and 6 ft (1.8 m) wide. Attached to two posts connected by a crossbar is a white nylon net. A marked area, called the goal crease, in front of the goal cage designates the area in which the goalie may operate.

Two blue lines stretch across the ice 60 ft (18 m) from each goal line, dividing the rink into three sections—the defensive zone, where the team defends its goal cage; the neutral zone, in the middle; and the attacking zone, where a team tries to shoot the puck into the opponent's net.

Nine circles indicate places where play resumes after a halt: the blue center circle in the middle of the ice; four other circles, two in each end near the goal area; and four additional face-off circles inside the center neutral zone. The opposing squads sit on benches behind the sideboards in the neutral zone. On the opposite side of the ice (directly across from the players' benches) is the penalty box, where a player must sit if he or she commits an infraction.

To advance the puck, players use a wooden or aluminum stick with a blade at the end. The blades may be no longer than 12.5 inches (31.8 centimeters). The length of the stick generally extends from the player's chin to the ice. Goaltenders, or goalies, use a stick with a broader surface. The disk-shaped puck is made of vulcanized rubber 3 inches (7.6 cm) in diameter and 1 inch (2.5 cm) thick. The puck weighs about 6 ounces (170 grams).

The players' uniforms consist of a shirt, knee-length pants held up with suspenders, stockings, heavy leather gloves, skates, and a helmet. Protective equipment, such as elbow and hip pads, is often used. Goaltenders also wear face masks, chest pads, and padded gloves to help them block shots that can approach speeds of 100 miles per hour (160 kilometers per hour).

Each team can have six players on the ice at any one time: a goaltender, two defenders, one center, and two forwards. The game begins at center ice with a face-off—the official drops the puck and the opposing centers attempt to gain control. The team with the puck tries to advance it into their opponent's zone and shoot it into the net for a goal. One player may skate with the puck the length of the ice to the other team's goal area, or several players may pass it back and forth as they skate toward the goal. It is illegal to kick the puck or use hands to advance it.

A team scores one point each time a player shoots the puck into the rival's net. The team with the most goals wins the game.

When a player is sent to the penalty box for committing a major infraction, the team must play shorthanded while the player sits in the penalty box. For minor infractions, such as tripping or holding an opponent,

The goalie for the Czech Republic Olympic ice hockey team dives to block a shot. The Czech team won Olympic gold in 1998.

a player must sit in the penalty box for two minutes. Major infractions, such as fighting or a flagrant foul, result in penalties of five minutes. If the opposing team scores a goal during the two-minute penalty, the player may leave the penalty box and resume play.

In rare cases, a referee may call a penalty shot. This happens when an attacking player is pulled down from behind as he nears the goal area. While the other ten athletes watch from the side, the player who has been tripped is allowed to skate toward the opponent's goalie and take one shot.

In the Olympics

The U.S. Olympic hockey team celebrates after winning the gold at the 1980 games.

Ice hockey was first played in the Olympics in 1920 as part of the Summer Games in Antwerp, Belgium. In 1924, it was included as one of the sports for the first Winter Games. Canada ruled Olympic hockey by taking the gold medal in six of the first seven Olympic competitions. During that time, Canadians compiled a record of 37 wins, 1 loss, and 3 ties, and outscored their opponents 403-34.

Teams from the United States and Europe, especially from the former Soviet Union, gradually challenged Canada's dominance. In 1956, the Soviet Union ended Canada's era of supremacy by winning a gold medal. Other than a surprising loss in 1960 to an American squad, Soviet skaters won every hockey gold medal for the next two decades.

The Soviet winning streak came to a stunning end in 1980 at the hands of the United States. The American team had been soundly beaten by the Soviet squad in an exhibition game a few days before the Olympics, so very few people expected much from the Americans. Coach Herb

Brooks, from the University of Minnesota, was optimistic. He enforced a strict regimen on his players, who he believed could do better than their seventh-place seed (out of the 12 teams).

The Americans surprised everyone by advancing to the second round to play against the powerful Soviet team. Before the game, the dynamic Brooks gathered his team and told his players, "You're meant to be here. This moment is yours." Brooks's determination that destiny awaited them invigorated the young squad. Trailing only 3-2 after two periods, the Americans skated with a vengeance, scored two goals, and held off repeated Soviet attacks to take away a 4-3 victory. Two days later the team defeated Finland to win the gold medal.

A worldwide audience viewed the spectacular game on television, labeled as the "miracle on ice." When Brooks left the dressing room after the game, state police assigned to guard the hallways stood with tears streaming down their faces.

The Soviet Union returned to form by winning the next two Olympic Games in 1984 and 1988. After the dissolution of the Soviet Union, members from the post-Cold War Unified Team captured yet another medal in 1992. Sweden took the gold medal in 1994. At the Nagano games in 1998, the team from the Czech Republic took top honors.

A GOALIE BAR NONE

American goalie Jim Craig was one of the stars of the dramatic 1980 hockey victory over the Soviet Union. Of 39 shots that came his way, Craig turned away 36, many in the last frenzied minutes of the final period when the Soviets mounted a furious charge in an attempt to salvage the game. With only eight minutes remaining, Craig made a desperate save with his skate on a wicked backhand shot by Vladimir Golikov. Then, with only 57 seconds left, Craig kicked aside another shot from point-blank range. United States coach Herb Brooks told reporters, "He was a tower of strength for us, no question. For an American team to be successful, the catalyst has to be the goalkeep."

LUGE

Luge is one of the most exciting and fastest-growing sports in the Winter Olympics. The high speeds, 70 to 80 miles per hour (112.6 to 128.7 kilometers per hour) on the treacherous courses, push athletes to perform at the top of their skills and provide tremendous thrills for spectators.

Origin of the Sport

Luge is relatively new to the Olympic world. It has, however, a long history in many regions of Europe, particularly in Germany, France, and Alpine countries. The word *luge* comes from the French word meaning "sled."

Norwegian writers first mentioned sled racing in 1480, and other references to the sport exist in the tales and writings of other European lands. The first international luge race was held in 1883, when 21 athletes from seven nations met in the Swiss resort of Davos. The race took place on a 2.5-mile (4-kilometer) stretch of road connecting St. Wolfgang to Klosters.

At first, luge competition came under the jurisdiction of the International Bobsleigh and Tobogganing Federation. In 1953, a separate governing body was established, and luge appeared as an event 11 years later at the Winter Games in Innsbruck, Austria.

One of the earliest luge superstars was Thomas Kohler of East Germany, who dominated the sport in the 1960s. He was the first athlete to win the world men's singles title three times (1962, 1964, and 1967) and Olympic gold medals in 1964 and 1968.

Competing in the Event

Downhill luge courses consist of an ice-covered surface and banked sides to prevent a sled from skidding off the course. Courses must be at least 1,094 yards (1,000 meters) for the men's events and 875 yds (800 m) for the women's events.

Each course offers a variety of challenges that force lugers to display their skills. In the straight sections, the sled builds up

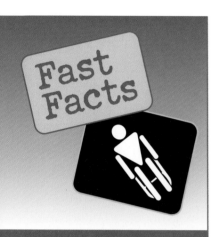

Fast Facts

First Olympic competition

Innsbruck, Austria; 1964

Legendary athletes

Georg Hackl, **Germany**
Manfred Schmid, **Austria**
Vera Zozulya, **Soviet Union**

Criteria for winning

Fastest time

speeds that may approach 75 miles per hour (120 km/h). Then come the gradually curving right-hand and left-hand bends. Farther down the course lies a hairpin bend, an extremely sharp turn designed to test the contestants' abilities to control their sleds. A bend shaped like an S and a more gradual-turning feature called a labyrinth are the final challenges of each run.

Athletes compete on a small sled made of fiberglass or wood fastened atop two runners. Sleds are usually 4 feet (1.2 m) long, 20 inches (51 cm) wide, 8 inches (20 cm) high, and weigh about 50 pounds (23 kilograms) for one-person sleds and 55 lbs (25 kg) for two-person sleds.

The luger lies on his or her back with feet extending beyond the front of the sled, shoulders resting on the seat in the rear, with head held up. Since the riders are on their backs, they steer the sled by applying leg and foot pressure on the runners and by exerting downward pressure on the sled with their shoulders. The pressure exerted against the athlete as the sled speeds down the course and zooms around the curves is twice the force exerted against an astronaut during a shuttle launch. Mechanical devices for steering or braking the luge are prohibited.

Participants must wear crash helmets to protect them from injuries. Most competitors also attach a form-fitting face shield to the front of the helmet. This shatterproof shield serves two purposes. It protects the athlete's face and also cuts down on wind resistance, leading to improved racing times. Skin-tight stretch suits also cut down on wind resistance. Gloves with small spikes help the racer push off at the start.

Athletes begin their runs by gripping the handles, rocking the sled back and forth, pulling off the handles, and shooting forward down the start ramp. Once underway, the athletes must remain on their backs for the duration of the race. A red light at the starting position indicates that the athlete must wait until the previous competitor has cleared the course. When the light turns green, the athlete has 30 seconds to begin in singles events and 45 seconds in doubles competition.

The luge requires four runs down the course in both men's and women's singles, but only two runs in the doubles competition. The Olympic doubles is open to either

A LOW POINT IN LUGE COMPETITION

The 1968 games produced one of the most unusual, and shameful, results in Olympic history. East German women had long excelled at the women's singles, so their first-, second-, and fourth-place finishes were not a surprise. Some astute observers, however, suspected the women were cheating, because they arrived with their sleds moments before the race and then quickly disappear after the race ended. When officials examined the sleds, they found that the runners had been illegally heated, which made the sleds run faster over the ice surface. The three East Germans were disqualified, and the gold medal went to Erica Lechner of Italy.

Lugers steer their sleds by exerting leg pressure on the runners and shifting their weight at the right moment.

same-sex or mixed pairs. The heavier athlete lies in the top seat, while the lighter partner stretches out in the bottom seat. In all events, the winner is the individual or team that accumulates the lowest total time for all runs.

In the Olympics

When the luge competition was added to the Winter Olympics for the 1964 games in Innsbruck, Austria, critics charged that the sport was too dangerous. They pointed to the lightning speeds that frequently resulted in spectacular, and sometimes deadly, crashes. A horrid confirmation of their fears occurred two weeks before the games opened. A British luger died following a crash in a practice run. The event went on as scheduled, and safety features added over the years have dramatically reduced the number of injuries.

Athletes from the former East Germany dominated the event in the early years of Olympic competition. In the first four games starting in 1964, East German lugers took 10 of the 12 medal spots in the men's single, 3 gold and a bronze in the doubles, and 7 of the 12 medals in the women's competition.

In more recent years, German and Austrian athletes have dominated the sport, led by Germany's GEORG HACKL, who has won three gold medals and one silver in the men's singles.

The Americans' role in the luge has grown in recent years. In 1964, the U.S. luge team was made up mainly of American soldiers stationed in Europe. As might be expected, they failed to contend for a medal. In 1979, however, the United States built the first refrigerated run (at Lake Placid), creating optimism for the future of the luge in America. Duncan Kennedy, winner of several World Cup titles, seemed ready to take on the Europeans in the race for the gold medal in the 1992 games, but he finished a distant tenth. Six years later at Nagano, Japan, two American teams did succeed, earning silver and bronze medals in the doubles event.

NORDIC SKIING

Nordic skiing consists of two main styles of snow skiing—cross-country skiing and ski jumping. The term *Nordic* refers to northern Europe, particularly the nations of Norway, Sweden, and Finland, where these forms of skiing originated.

◄ **SEE HISTORY OF SKIING ON PAGE 18.**

Origin of the Sport

Skiing had a military purpose long before it became a sport. In the 900s, Norwegian soldiers promoted the use of skis by specially trained ski patrols that guarded the nation's vast stretches of snow-covered forests and fields. Historical records tell of the battle of Ilsen in Norway in 1200, during which the King of Sweden employed ski troops.

Six years later a race was initiated to memorialize two brave soldiers on skis who prevented the capture of the king's young son by whisking him across snow-covered mountains. The race is called the Birkebeinerrennet (Birchleg) race because the soldiers wrapped their legs with birch bark to protect them from the cold. The cross-country event follows the same 35-mile (56-kilometer) route used to rescue the young prince.

Sweden has its counterpart to the Birchleg race, the annual 53-mile (85-km) Vasaloppet cross-country marathon. At the start of the 1500s, a young political leader named Gustav Vasa attempted unsuccessfully to stir his reluctant countrymen to rebel against Denmark, which then controlled his land. When Danish troops came to arrest Vasa, he fled into the countryside and headed for neighboring Norway.

After his escape, the Swedes decided Vasa had been right to try to unite people against the Danes. Two woodsmen headed into the wilderness to try and bring him back. They caught up with Vasa as he neared the Norwegian border and persuaded him to return. Vasa then organized an army, defeated the Danes, and was elected King Gustavas Eriksson I in June 1523.

More than 400 years later, a newspaper editor, Anders Pers, proposed the nation commemorate the event by staging

Fast Facts

First Olympic competition

Cross-Country Skiing
Men's
Chamonix, France; 1924
Women's
Oslo, Norway; 1952

Ski Jumping
Chamonix, France; 1924

Legendary athletes

Cross-Country Skiing
Björn Daehlie, **Norway**
Thorleif Haug, **Norway**
Sixten Jernberg, **Sweden**
Galina Kulakova, **Soviet Union**
Raisa Smetanina, **Soviet Union**

Ski Jumping
Espen Bredesen, **Norway**
Masahiko Harada, **Japan**
Matti Nykänen, **Finland**

Criteria for winning

Cross-Country Skiing
Fastest time

Ski Jumping
Highest score

HUNTER ON SKIS

Early Norse myths include references to skiing. The Finnish epic *Kalevala* recounts the heroics of a hunter.

"In his hands his pole
 grasped firmly,
On the left shoe glided
 forward,
And pushed onward
 with his right one.
Chased the elk upon
 his show shoes."

a ski race along the same route. In explaining the purpose for such a lengthy race, Pers noted, "It may seem long, but that is as it should be: a real test of man's ability to stand up to hardship." The first Vasaloppet race was held on March 19, 1922. Ernst Alm defeated 118 other competitors by completing the marathon in a little over 7 hours, 32 minutes, to take the memorial cup.

Skis were used by the military forces of various nations. Sweden fielded armies on skis and snowshoes as early as 1521, and Norway trained soldiers to move in unison on skis. In 1767, the Norwegian military conducted its first races on skis, 76 years before the civilian sector organized its first ski competition.

The "Father of Ski Jumping," Sondre Nordheim of Norway, introduced the sport of ski jumping in 1860 when he executed the first officially measured jump. Six years later his improved bindings, which wrapped around the heel and gave athletes more control over their skis, enabled competitors to jump greater distances.

The first mention of a ski jump took place in 1879 when a group of athletes gathered at Huseby Hill, Norway. While most competitors cautiously descended the slope to the jumping-off point, a group of skiers from Telemark Valley raced down the slope, soared into the air, and landed 76 feet (122 km) away.

According to one observer, "The Huseby slope was one which, only a few years previously, had been described as highly dangerous and impossible to descend when snow was fast and in good condition. Every man [except the men from Telemark] carried a long, stout staff, and on that, so they thought, their lives depended. Starting from the summit, riding their poles, as in former times, like witches on broomsticks, checking the speed with frantic efforts, they slipped downwards to the dreaded platform from which they were supposed to leap, but over which they trickled, as it were. But then came the Telemark boys, erect at starting, pliant, confident, without anything but a fir branch in their hands, swooping downwards with ever-increasing impetus, until, with a bound, they were in the air, and 76 feet of space was cleared ere, with a resounding smack, their ski touched the slippery slope beneath and they shot onwards to the plain, where suddenly they turned, stopped in a smother of snow-dust and faced the hill they had just descended!"

Polar explorer Fridtjof Nansen added more favorable publicity to Nordic skiing in 1888 by crossing Greenland on skis. His subsequent best-selling book introduced the sport to millions around the world.

In 1910, the Norwegian Ski Federation organized the first international ski congress. Shortly before the first Winter Olympics in 1924, the group reorganized, calling itself the International Ski Federation.

Scandinavian immigrants introduced Nordic skiing to the United States in the late 1800s when they settled in the Midwest and northern New England. They held the first National Championship in Michigan in 1904, but American skiing did not attract a strong following until the automobile provided travel to ski areas. Construction of ski resorts followed.

During World War II (1939–1945), Finnish soldiers on skis fought off the invading Soviet army and caused the vastly superior enemy some unexpected problems. When the United States entered the war, American ski troops successfully battled the Germans in Italy's towering mountains. Cross-country skiing became more popular after the war, especially in the United States.

Competing in the Event

Olympic Nordic skiing includes five racing events and five jumping events for men and five racing events for women. The five racing events for men at the 1998 Winter Olympics in Nagano, Japan, were the 10-kilometer classical, the 15-kilometer freestyle pursuit, the 30-kilometer classical, the 50-kilometer freestyle, and the 4 x 10-kilometer relay. Women competed in the 5-kilometer classical, the 10-kilometer freestyle pursuit, the 15-kilometer classical, the 30-kilometer freestyle, and the 4 x 5-kilometer relay.

Classical and freestyle refer to the style skiers use to glide across the course. The classical form has been used since the sport began. In this form the athlete advances by alternately thrusting the skis forward in parallel kicks. The skier gains additional momentum and balance from ski poles.

East German skier Gerhard Grimmer first used the free-style method in 1971, but this form did not become popular until 1982, when American skier Bill Koch perfected the technique. Somewhat similar to ice skating, the freestyle method differs from the classical in that the skier pushes off diagonally from the inside edge of the ski that bears the skier's weight. This provides extra power and kick and enables the skier to glide across the snow more rapidly. Purists labeled the freestyle method as altering the basic nature of Nordic skiing, but Olympic officials permitted the form at the 1988 games in Calgary, Canada.

In the four individual races, skiers leave the starting area every 30 seconds and are rated on how long it takes to complete the course. The winner is the athlete who posts the fastest time. Relay races, in which four skiers compete as a

Competitors in cross-country events gain speed by sliding one ski forward while kicking out sideways with the other ski and pushing off with their poles.

team, use a mass start in which the first competitor from each team kicks off at the same time. He or she then skis toward the exchange zone, where the second competitor takes over. Instead of exchanging a baton, as in track and field events, the athlete entering the exchange zone must touch the body of his or her teammate. The team posting the fastest time wins the event.

Pursuit races (15 kilometers for men, 10 kilometers for women) are run in two heats. In the first, skiers leave individually and compete against the clock. The finishing times then determine the position for the second heat. For example, if a skier finished first by 3 seconds, he or she receives a 3-second head start over the second-place finisher. The competitors are arranged in this manner through the entire field.

Officials try to set up a course that consists of one-third flat terrain, one-third uphill, and one-third downhill. Rather than winding only through flat, open stretches, the course winds through wooded areas as well. Sudden changes of direction, sharp turns, and difficult downhill plunges are avoided so the athletes can maintain their rhythm. The highest point of a course typically does not exceed 5,414 feet (1,650 meters), and there are no long downhill runs in the final sections of the course. The track is usually 12 to 18 ft (3.6 to 5.5 m) wide.

Nordic skis are made from fiberglass, hardwood, or aluminum. Though sturdy, the skis are lightweight and flexible, and they curve slightly upward at the tip for ease of motion across the surface of the snow. Most skilled athletes use skis that are about 1 foot (30 centimeters) longer than their height.

Like the equipment for other skiing events, the boots are made from plastic or hard leather. The ski bindings hold the boots to the skis and are designed to release the skis whenever the athlete falls. The athlete uses ski poles made of fiberglass, aluminum, steel, or bamboo. The ski poles end in a sharp point surrounded by a circular webbed ring (the basket), which prevents the pole from sinking deep into the snow. Skiers hold a rubber or plastic grip at the top of the pole.

Cross-country skiers wear less clothing than downhill skiers to allow greater freedom of movement. Over thermal underwear and long wool hose, the skier typically wears knee breeches, a shirt, a sweater, and an insulated parka, plus goggles, a hat or headband, and gloves.

Currently only male athletes compete in the five Olympic jumping contests. Jumpers compete in three individual events—the small hill (70 meters, or 230 feet) and the large hill (90 meters, or 296 feet) events, as well as the individual Nordic combined, which requires the competitors to both jump and ski in a 15-kilometer race. A team jumping event and the team nordic combined complete the events. The 70- or 90-meter measurement refers to the distance from the takeoff point at the end of the ski ramp to the norm point, which is the start of the competitors' expected landing area. The norm point is clearly marked on each side of the landing area.

Jumping competitions provide some of the most exciting moments in Nordic skiing. The athlete skis down a long ramp called the in-run, soars into the air with as much spring as possible in the takeoff, and then strains forward to reach maximum length for the jump before settling onto the out-run—the landing slope that angles downward and away from the skier.

Athletes receive points for distance and style, which includes the form while the jumper is in the air and his balance on landing. Jumpers lean forward into a horizontal position almost parallel to the skis, with their skis pointed outward in a V shape to take advantage of air currents. Their arms are tightly held at their sides to reduce air resistance. Moments before landing, the jumper straightens up so that the skis are immediately under him. This is called the telemark position—named after the Norse skiers from the Telemark Valley who originated the maneuver—with one foot in front of the other and the knees half-bent to absorb the shock. Some jumpers have spanned well over 300 ft (91 m)—greater than the length of a football field.

Judges deduct points for improper arm position, skis crisscrossing in the air, and other errors. The most serious fault occurs when a jumper falls after landing. Five judges score each attempt. The highest and lowest marks are dropped from consideration, and the other three are added together to arrive at the athlete's final score.

Each athlete makes two jumps in the individual events. The athlete with the highest point total after two rounds is declared the winner. In team events, four athletes jump for each nation, and the top three scores in each of the two rounds are added. The team with the highest point total wins.

For years, athletes jumped in the classical form, with their skis parallel to each other. In the 1980s, this style was gradually replaced by the V-shaped method. At first officials hesitated to accept the change, but by the 1994 Olympics in Lillehammer, Norway, all contestants were using the V.

In the individual combined, athletes compete in a jump on one day and a 15-kilometer race the next day. Three men from each team compete on a 90-meter hill in the team combined and then engage in a 30-kilometer relay.

Clothing provides maximum warmth while adding minimal weight. Over thermal underwear and socks, the jumper wears stretch pants, a shirt, a sweater, and an insulated parka, plus goggles, a hat or headband, and gloves. Jumping skis are the longest in the sport, typically measuring 94 inches (239 cm) in length.

Casey Colby of the 1998 U.S. team at Nagano demonstrated how wind can affect the outcome of this event. As he lifted off the ramp into the air on his second jump, a strong gust of wind hit him from the side and smacked his right ski downward. He later recalled the moment: "I don't know what

Long, steep ramps enable ski jumpers to attain maximum distance.

happened. I thought I was going to the bottom but all of a sudden—boom—and my ski's down and so am I." All the preparation and training counted for nothing in the face of a sudden whim of nature.

American jumpers face not only obstacles posed by nature, but also a lack of interest in the sport by their countrymen, who prefer watching football, baseball, and other sporting events. As a high school student, Mike Keuler trained almost every day in the ski jump, but his friends refused to believe that he would rather ski jump than play hockey. "A lot of hockey players didn't take what I did seriously," explained Keuler. "Not many people realized, especially some of my best friends at home, how seriously I did it."

In the Olympics

Nordic events for men appeared in the first Winter Olympic Games in Chamonix, France, in 1924. Norwegian athletes dominated the one jumping event (90-meter hill), two cross-country races (18-kilometer and 50-kilometer), and one individual combined event by capturing 10 of the 12 medal positions. Women's competition was not included until 1952, when a 10-kilometer cross-country event was staged. Finland swept all three medals in the initial race.

Thorleif Haug of Norway won gold medals in 1924—the 18-kilometer, 50-kilometer, and the combined, as well as a bronze medal in the 90-meter jump. In 1974, researchers discovered that a scoring error had given the bronze medal to Haug instead of American skier Anders Haugen. Officials remedied the mistake and held a special ceremony in Oslo, where the 83-year-old Haugen finally received his bronze medal.

In the first Winter Olympics, Norway's athletes showed the world that they intended to reign supreme in Nordic events. Along with other Scandinavian countries, such as Sweden and Finland, the Norwegians have consistently placed at or near the top. In recent years, superb competitors such as BJöRN DAEHLIE continue to earn medals for Norway.

At the 1928 games in St. Moritz, Switzerland, athletes were reminded that weather often dictates the outcomes of

Nordic competition. With the temperature near zero, contestants in the 50-kilometer race waxed their skis in the morning and prepared for the race. By the time the first athlete kicked off, however, the temperature had soared to near 70°F (21°C) and turned the course to slush. The winning time was more than one hour longer than the 1924 result.

One athlete at the 1928 games skied almost too well. In the ski jump, Jacob Tullin Thams of Norway jumped 240 ft (73 m) and outdistanced his closest competitor by 43 ft (13 m). Unfortunately, since 1924 Olympic athletes posted no jump longer than 161 ft (49 m), the hill had been set up to handle jumps of 213 ft (65 m) and less. Thams landed far beyond the safety zone and sustained serious injuries when he crashed to the ground. Adding to his misfortune, the judges penalized him so heavily in style points that the hapless skier fell to 28th place.

World War II caused the cancellation of the Olympic Games in 1940 and 1944. The conflict nearly destroyed the career of Birger Ruud of Norway. The ski jumper had captured gold medals in 1932 and 1936. When Adolf Hitler's armies invaded his homeland in 1940, Ruud was arrested and thrown into a concentration camp. He languished there under miserable conditions until the war ended in 1945. He returned to skiing in the 1948 games held in St. Moritz, Switzerland. The 36-year-old Ruud served as coach of the Norwegian team, but when the weather turned nasty the night before the ski jump, he substituted himself for a less experienced athlete. The man who had endured extreme hardship during the war years summoned his reserves to place second and earn a silver medal.

Two athletes dominated the Nordic events in the 1950s and early 1960s—Finland's Veikko Hakulinen and Sweden's "king of skis," Sixten Jernberg. Hakulinen, who almost failed to make his first games because he had accidentally gashed his leg with an axe while chopping wood, first gained Olympic fame with a gold medal in the 50-kilometer race in 1952. He won six more medals in cross-country events in the following two Winter Games. In three Olympics, Jernberg won nine medals, including four gold medals.

In 1960, Hakulinen was responsible for one of the most exciting moments in the relay, the only Nordic competition

BJÖRN DAEHLIE KEEPS THE FAITH

Cross-country skier extraordinaire, Norway's Björn Daehlie compiled an unmatched Olympic record over the span of three separate games. In an interview for a skiing newsletter, Daehlie explained how he achieved his tremendous success: "I have been lucky and avoided injuries and overtraining through my career. I feel this is because I have been patient with my training, have taken my time and have made appropriate increases [in amounts of training]. Also, you need to keep the faith with your training because you will have some heavy, harder periods. All athletes meet setbacks sooner or later! It's part of your training as skiers to tolerate these down periods and then come back again stronger! I keep my energy reserves high by taking time to hunt and fish with my friends. We all need to get away from training now and then."

BILL KOCH

Until Bill Koch from Guilford, Vermont, came along, no United States athlete had won a medal in cross-country skiing. When he entered the 1976 games, Koch and the other American athletes were expected to continue the unspectacular tradition and place well down in the pack.

Koch reversed that with his finish in the 30-kilometer race. For a time, the American led the long-distance event, but Soviet skier Sergei Saveliev overtook him to take the gold medal. Koch, drawing on his last reserves in the race's final stretch, held off Saveliev's teammate, Ivan Garanin, to earn a silver medal, the first medal in cross-country for the United States.

that pits athlete against athlete instead of each skier kicking off individually and racing against the clock. The Swedish team sped to an early 7-second lead by the end of the first leg, but fell into third place behind Finland and Norway at the midpoint. Norwegians appeared to have the event sewed up when they built a commanding 20-second lead with one leg to go, but six-time Olympic medalist Hakulinen had other thoughts. The outstanding athlete, appearing in his final event of his last Olympics, summoned every ounce of mental and physical strength, overtook his Norwegian opponent, and skied to victory only three feet ahead of his rival.

Superb female athletes added their names to the list of Olympic stars in Nordic events. Galina Kulakova of the former Soviet Union won four gold, two silver, and two bronze medals between 1968 and 1980, highlighted by her sweep of all three women's events in 1972 (5-kilometer, 10-kilometer, and relay). She would have won nine medals, but judges disqualified her bronze medal performance in the 5-kilometer event in 1976 because she had used a nasal spray that contained a banned substance.

Juha Mieto of Finland experienced misfortune of his own in the 15-kilometer race. In 1972, he barely missed the bronze medal by a margin of .06 seconds. As if that were not enough, he returned in 1980 to compete in the same event and missed the gold medal by only .01 seconds. Since then the rules have been changed in cross-country races so that times are rounded to the nearest full second.

Athletes from other nations gradually challenged Scandinavian teams for supremacy on the ski ramps and along country trails. German and Soviet skiers regularly won medals, and athletes from Japan and the United States posted impressive performances in the 1970s.

Japan, which had previously won only one medal in the Winter Games, bested the Scandinavian nations in 1972 in Sapporo, Japan. Competing before thousands of Japanese spectators, Yukio Kasaya leaped to a gold medal in the 70-meter jump. The entire nation rejoiced when his teammates, Akitsugu Konno and Seiji Aochi, captured the silver and bronze medals for a clean sweep. When asked later about the secret to his successful jumps, gold medalist Kasaya answered, "Challenge not your rivals, but yourself."

American skier Bill Koch surprised everyone at the 1976 games by skiing to a silver medal in the 30-kilometer event. It was the best finish by an American in the cross-country events. Only one American athlete before him—Anders Haugen in the 90-meter ski jump in 1924—had won a bronze medal in the Nordic skiing events.

Koch had to overcome a serious health problem simply to reach the Olympics. Since he suffered from exercise-induced asthma, Koch took medication regularly and had to watch carefully how much he pushed himself. As a result, few observers gave Koch much of a chance to finish in the top six, let alone win a medal. Determined to prove his doubters wrong, Koch skied a spirited race and handed his country its first cross-country medal.

Unfortunately, since Nordic events were not popular in the United States, no American press or television reporters waited at the finish line to record the moment of triumph. People in Koch's hometown of Guilford, Vermont, however, collected enough money to send his mother and brother to Austria so they could watch Koch compete in his next two races. The American skier could not duplicate his victory for his family, and finished 13th in the 50-kilometer event and 6th in the 15-kilometer race.

In the 1980s, MATTI NYKÄNEN of Finland captured successive gold medals in the 90-meter jump, won a silver and a gold in the 70-meter jump, and earned a fourth gold medal by helping his teammates win the 1988 team jump. Marja-Liisa Hämäläinen of Finland became the first woman to win three individual gold medals in 1984, with victories in the 5-kilometer, 10-kilometer, and 20-kilometer races.

The greatest female athlete in the 1980s, and possibly in the history of the Winter Games, was Soviet skier Raisa Smetanina. Her ten medals over five Olympics—three in 1976, two in 1980, two in 1984, two in 1988, and one in 1992—were the most won in the Winter Olympics by a woman. They included four gold, five silver, and one bronze.

Other nations continued to provide strong challenges to Scandinavians in the 1990s. Japan and Finland have become top contenders in jumping events, while Italy, Germany, and Russia have established themselves as strong performers in Nordic events.

Angling his skis into a V formation, Japanese ski jumper Kazuyoshi Funaki sails his way to a gold medal at the 1998 games in Nagano, Japan.

Björn Daehlie led a talented pack of Nordic athletes as the millennium approached. The gifted skier raced to 12 medals through 1998, and he has set his sights on the 2002 games in Salt Lake City, Utah. Daehlie posted a total of four medals in 1992, 1994, and 1998.

Espen Bredesen of Norway learned that the experience of bitter defeat can make the task of working toward victory even sweeter. He was the subject of much criticism and snickering by athletes after finishing last in the 90-meter jump in 1992. Since Bredesen came from Norway, which takes immense pride in its athletes and expects medal-winning races and jumps, he felt embarrassed to have finished far behind his teammates. Fans called him "Espen the Eagle" in a derogatory comparison to British jumper Eddie Edwards, who was so inept on the slopes that he gained the sarcastic nickname "Eddie the Eagle."

Instead of giving up, Bredesen pushed himself to perfect the V technique in time for the games in Lillehammer. His intense work paid off when he won a gold medal in the 70-meter event and a silver medal in the 90-meter jump. He later explained that he won because of his training, focus, and determination to make up for his dismal performance in 1992: "The world could have fallen apart around me, and I wouldn't have noticed. I felt very aggressive and was really ready to win." Defeat in one Olympics powered Bredesen to victory in the next.

Manuela Di Centa of Italy also overcame obstacles to triumph in the Olympic Games. After performing poorly at the games in Albertville in 1992, Di Centa decided to consult her doctor. For some unexplained reason she was feeling weak and listless instead of her usual energetic self. The physician put her in a hospital, where she spent two months recovering from a thyroid disorder. A reinvigorated Di Centa left the hospital with the goal of doing better than her 1992 showing, and she surpassed her fondest wishes with a sterling performance in 1994. Di Centa grabbed a medal in each of the five women's events, including gold medals in the 15-kilometer and 30-kilometer races, silver in the 5-kilometer and 10-kilometer, and a bronze in the team relay. The heroic athlete hoped her achievement would influence others: "I want little girls to be inspired by seeing that a woman can win in sports. I think my medals touch all women."

The Japanese team at Nagano in 1998 demonstrated that even though athletes train for years in order to participate, a little luck is always welcome. Shortly before the Nagano Olympics, Japanese skier Kazuyoshi Funaki competed in an Austrian cross-country event. An executive from a ski company handed the athlete a potato and explained that Austrians consider the potato a good luck charm. When Funaki won his event, he asked the executive to bring an even larger potato to the Nagano Games for the whole team. The executive presented the team with a potato about the size of a bowling ball, and before each Nordic event, the Japanese gathered around the potato and held it in their hands.

Apparently, sentiment only went so far. After the Japanese skiers won a gold medal in the team relay, someone asked the executive if the team would preserve the lucky potato in a trophy case. "No, they ate it," was the answer.

Masahiko Harada was haunted by his disappointing finish in 1994 when his poor jump in the team ski jumping competition cost the team a gold medal. Four years later Harada turned the tables by helping his team to victory in the large hill event with an outstanding jump. After his heroics, an ecstatic Harada repeatedly exclaimed, "I did it! I did it!"

Despite his excellent performance, Harada still could not erase from his memory the bitter experience of 1994: "We have won the gold medal this time, but the memory of what happened four years ago still weighs heavy. The fact that I did a terrible thing will not change."

The United States team still struggles to win Olympic medals in Nordic events. John Bauer has skied to gold medals in World Cup competition, and Nina Kemppel from Alaska poses a threat on the women's side, but they continue to live in the shadows of the powerful European teams.

SHORT TRACK SKATING

Unlike long track speed skating, which usually pairs skaters in heats, in short track speed skating four to six skaters compete together. Spectators love the fast-paced events, which often involve contact between skaters and occasional spills.

◀ **SEE HISTORY OF SKATING ON PAGE 47.**

Origin of the Sport

Short track speed skating is a recent addition to the array of speed skating events. Short track caught on in Europe, Korea, Canada, and the United States in the latter half of the 20th century. Like all speed skating events, short track traces its roots back thousands of years, when Europeans raced each other on frozen canals and lakes.

Competing in the Event

Short track skates are molded to the foot and have extra padding in the ankles to give support for quick turns. To help the athlete lean into a turn, the blade on the left foot is set toward the outside of the boot, whereas the blade on the right skate rests closer to the inside. The blades are also more curved than in other types of skating because of the tight track.

The course used in short track speed skating is much smaller than in long track skating. The 364-foot (111-meter) indoor track is about the same in circumference as a hockey rink. To protect the athletes, padded walls encircle the rink. In addition, skaters wear hard helmets, gloves, knee pads, and shin guards.

The Winter Olympics offers six events in short track: 500-meter and 1,000-meter races for men and women, a men's 5,000-meter relay, and a women's 3,000-meter relay. Since all events are held on the same course, the number of laps distinguishes one event from another.

The 500-meter and 1,000-meter events feature heats of four skaters, with the top two finishers advancing to the next round. The winner is the individual who first crosses the finish line in the finals.

Fast Facts

First Olympic competition
Albertville, France; 1992

Legendary athletes
Chun Lee-Kyung, **South Korea**
Kim Ki-Hoon, **South Korea**
Cathy Turner, **USA**

Criteria for winning
Fastest time

HOW MANY LAPS?

The tight short track speed skating courses require athletes to complete many laps. This means skaters must maneuver around frequent curves and turns, which is not only hard on the ankles but also causes many collisions.

For each event, skaters must complete the following number of laps:

Race	Laps
500 meters	4.5
1,000 meters	9
3,000 meters	27
5,000 meters	45

Eight teams of four skaters compete in both relay events. Two heats are run, and the top two teams from each heat face off in the finals. The first racer of each team leads off the relay. The teams can determine how many laps each athlete skates, and they can exchange as often as they want. The only requirement is that each of the four skaters complete at least one lap, and that the exchange to the last skater take place before the last two full laps. Relay exchanges, which may take place at any part of the track, are completed when one skater touches a teammate.

The start of each race is important in short track speed skating. The skater who jumps out of the pack to a speedy lead can take the inside position. Skaters are allowed one false start, but a second one disqualifies the athlete and team.

Strategy is crucial. A skater must decide whether to vault to the lead and attempt to hold it from start to finish, or to jockey for position with the opponents and maintain a reserve of speed for the final few laps. Jumping off to an early lead has its advantages, but the skater in the lead position also faces more wind resistance. Holding back for a final push often works, but then the skater risks falling too far behind, being blocked in by other skaters, or being wiped out in a collision if anyone in front stumbles or falls.

Passing another skater is an art in itself. The rules state that passing must be done without bumping into a competitor. Any infraction means disqualification. Since the lead skater has the right of way, the offender is almost always the passing skater.

In the Olympics

Short track speed skating made its debut as an exhibition event at the 1988 games in Calgary, Canada. It was included as a medal sport four years later in Albertville, France, where a men's 1,000-meter individual event and a 5,000-meter relay, as well as a women's 500-meter individual event and 3,000-meter relay, were included. The men's 500-meter event and women's 1,000-meter event were added at Lillehammer, Norway, in 1994.

The Korean men's team took most of the medals in the first few Olympics in which the sport was included. They won all but one of the individual events and one of the three relay events. In the 5,000-meter relay in 1992, the Korean team edged out the Canadian squad when Kim Ki-Hoon threw himself across the finish line. Two years later, South Korea's Chae Ji-Hoon won a gold medal in the 500-meter and a silver in the 1,000-meter event.

Korean women have not fared as well as their male counterparts. The exception is CHUN LEE-KYUNG, who took gold medals in the 1,000-meter event in 1994 and 1998 as well as a bronze medal in the 500-meter race in 1998.

One woman who has made a mark in the sport, both for her talent and for her controversial style, is Cathy Turner of the United States. Turner won gold medals in the 500-meter event in Albertville and again in Lillehammer, but many skaters claimed she bumped them and attempted to throw them off balance. Some athletes were so angered by what they believed were Turner's unsportsmanlike tactics that they refused to shake her hand at the medals ceremony. The criticism may have had some effect, because the judges later disqualified Turner in the 1,000-meter event in 1994 for blocking another skater.

Turning so sharply that their fingertips skim the ice, short track speed skaters race toward the finish line.

SNOWBOARDING

Snowboarding, often called "riding the frozen wave," is a relative newcomer to winter activities, and one that enjoys immense popularity. The combination of surfing and skiing has drawn many outdoor enthusiasts to snow-covered hills and rises, particularly those who seek alternative thrills to downhill skiing.

Origin of the Sport

Snowboarding gained popularity in 1965 when Sherman Poppen of Vermont invented the Snurfer, skis adapted for surfing on snow. After watching his daughter try to slide down a hill while standing on her sled, Poppen fashioned a simple snowboard by bolting together a pair of children's skis and attaching a rope to the front. His invention was so popular that the other neighborhood children clamored for their own snowboards. Poppen's wife nicknamed the creation the Snurfer by combining the words *snow* and *surfer.*

Other athletes modified Poppen's board. A New Jersey teenager named Tom Sims created an improved version in 1969, and Jake Burton experimented with different variations of snowboards. Countless runs down Vermont slopes led to alterations in Burton's makeshift workshop. He discovered that wood worked better than plastic for the board's top surface, and that the board needed to have sharp edges for more accurate turns and quick stops. He applied a hard plastic to the bottom of the board to reduce friction on the snow, and he shortened the board. By the time he was finished, Burton had invented a snowboard capable of executing most of the moves that could be done on skis. His company, Burton Snowboards, is the largest producer of snowboards in the world.

The earliest snowboard competitions involved athletes who assembled at informal gatherings to snowboard and have fun. A festive air surrounded the events, which were not stifled by rules set down by international committees. Chris Karol, one of the top early snowboarders, said, "In the early days, nobody trained or did anything like that. We just showed up. It was something to do in the winter when you couldn't skateboard."

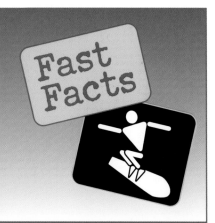

Fast Facts

First Olympic competition

Nagano, Japan; 1998

Legendary athletes

Ross Rebagliati, **Canada**

Karine Ruby, **France**

Gian Simmen, **Switzerland**

Nicola Thost, **Germany**

Criteria for winning

Highest score

Snowboarding encountered some bumps in the road in its development as a sport. Many resort owners regarded the sport as too dangerous and didn't welcome snowboarders on their ski slopes. They feared that snowboarders would disturb their regular ski customers and cause too many injuries.

More championships were staged for snowboarders as the 1980s approached. In 1988, the first World Cup of snowboarding was organized. Other events in Europe and North America offer challenges to top athletes, particularly the West Coast Snowboarding Championships at Lake Tahoe, California, and the National Snowsurfing Championship.

Competing in the Event

Very little equipment is required for snowboarding. Snowboards are made of laminated wood over foam centers that have steel edges for easier turning and navigating through the snow. They vary in length, although most are about 5 feet (1.5 meters). Snowboards used in the giant slalom are generally stiffer than those used in the halfpipe, which places a premium on flexibility to allow the athlete to perform aerial maneuvers. Bindings hold the snowboarder's feet in place, and a nylon band called a leash is strapped around the leg to prevent a snowboard from careening out of control.

Freestyle and beginner snowboarders generally use hard plastic high-back bindings that are fitted over soft boots. Other athletes prefer a plate binding, which is a metal or hard plastic plate with a toe and heel fastener.

Competitive snowboarding involves the halfpipe competition and the giant slalom race. In the halfpipe competition, athletes perform stunts in a ditch dug into the snow. The event receives its name from the ditch's appearance—a U-shape that resembles a pipe cut in half. The halfpipe stretches 250 to 350 ft (76 to 107 m) long with sides that rise anywhere from

A snowboarder performs maneuvers during a halfpipe competition.

7 to 14 ft (2 to 4 m) on each side. Snowboarders glide up and down the sides to gain momentum and then show daring and creativity by executing their stunts in front of judges. This event creates great excitement because each athlete is free to perform his or her own tricks.

Judges award points for how well the athletes perform their stunts. In the men's event, the top eight athletes advance to the finals after two rounds. In the women's event, the top four competitors advance to the finals. The winner is the individual who totals the highest number of points.

In the giant slalom, entrants start by pushing off a post driven into the snow, then race through a series of gates as they speed down a steep course. Unlike the halfpipe, which rewards creativity, the giant slalom requires speed and control. The athlete who completes the course in the fastest time without missing a gate is the winner.

In the Olympics

While most winter sports boast a proud heritage dating back hundreds, if not thousands, of years, snowboarding has existed for less than half a century. Its inclusion in the Olympics is even more recent. In 1995 officials of the International Olympic Committee announced that snowboarding would be a part of the 1998 Winter Games in Nagano, Japan. Four events were scheduled—the men's and women's giant slalom and the men's and women's halfpipe.

Snowboarders greeted the news with enthusiasm. According to Chris Karol, "The Olympics are going to do a lot for the sport. There's something about the Olympics that makes people pay attention. It will give kids something to aspire to. The sport is going to produce new role models for kids everywhere."

The United States team headed to Nagano as an early favorite, along with Austria, Germany, and the Scandinavian nations. In both the men's and women's halfpipe competitions, American athletes won bronze medals. GIAN SIMMEN of Switzerland captured the men's gold, while Germany's Nicola Thost won the women's gold medal. In the giant slalom, Ross Rebagliati of Canada won the men's gold medal, while Karine Ruby of France took the gold medal in the women's event.

SPEED SKATING

Unlike figure skating, which demands grace, precision, and athletic ability, speed skating requires strength, endurance, and quickness. Speed skating has often been compared to races and sprints in track and field events.

◀ **SEE HISTORY OF SKATING ON PAGE 47.**

Origin of the Sport

The sport of speed skating developed naturally when people used frozen waterways as roadways to travel across ice. Eventually two unknown skaters challenged one another to see who could skate faster, and speed skating was born.

Of the three types of skating—speed skating, figure skating, and hockey—speed skating was the first to be organized into a sport. The first speed skating races were held in the 1500s on frozen canals and waterways of Holland. Dutch skaters still race on the canals. The sport spread to the British Isles, where the Dutch introduced iron blades, the first significant technological innovation in skating, in 1572. Scottish speed skaters organized the Skating Club of Edinburgh in the 1700s. The first recorded speed skating competition took place in England on February 4, 1763. This spurred the formation of skating clubs throughout northern Europe. At first the competitions were among laborers. Aristocrats, who preferred to figure skate, judged the contests.

Speed skating was made popular in the United States by a famous family of speed skaters. T. Donoghue and his two sons used a longer blade that they attached to the boot, and shorter leg strokes, which enhanced speed. The Donoghues established numerous records in the latter half of the 1800s. Joseph Donoghue became the first American skater to break the three-minute mile.

The first speed skating club in the United States originated in Philadelphia in 1849, and skaters in New York and Washington soon followed suit. E. W. Bushnell of Philadelphia revolutionized the sport in 1850 by making the first all-steel skate. The more durable, lightweight steel blades led to faster times in speed races.

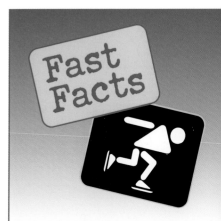

Fast Facts

First Olympic competition

Men's
Chamonix, France; 1924
Women's
Squaw Valley, California; 1960

Legendary athletes

Ivar Ballangrud, **Norway**
Bonnie Blair, **USA**
Eric Heiden, **USA**
Irving Jaffee, **USA**
Dan Jansen, **USA**
Johann Olav Koss, **Norway**
Lydia Skoblikova, **Soviet Union**
Clas Thunberg, **Finland**

Criteria for winning

Fastest time

Dutch skaters introduced the format that is used today in long track events, including the idea of a double track and races of varying lengths. The first World Championships were held in 1889, when the Netherlands hosted a competition involving the champions of four nations. Jaap Eden of Holland was crowned the first "Champion of the World." American skaters staged 10- and 20-mile races in the late 1870s and hosted their first national championship in 1891.

Norwegian speed skaters monopolized international racing until the 1920s. Today, American, Russian, and Scandinavian athletes excel on the ice. In the United States, the sport is governed by the Amateur Skating Union of the United States.

Competing in the Event

The long, narrow blades—up to 6 inches longer than those of figure skaters—help speed skaters attain speeds of 35 miles per hour (56 kilometers). Measuring only ½ inch in thickness and 12 to 18 inches (30 to 46 centimeters) in length, the longer steel blade assists the skaters since more metal comes into contact with the surface of the ice. A speed skater's boots do not extend as far up the ankle as a figure skate.

Many athletes have begun using a new skate called the slap, or clap, skate. Invented by the Dutch, the slap skate features boot heels that separate from the blades as the skater glides along the ice and then slap back in place when the foot leaves the ice. At the 1998 games in Nagano, Japan, the slap skate enabled Dutch skater Gianni Romme to cut more than 15 seconds off the world record in the 10,000-meter event.

The man whose record Romme broke, legendary speed skater and three-time gold medal winner at the 1994 Olympics in Lillehammer, JOHANN OLAV KOSS, tested the new skates. The retired competitor was won over. "They're fun," he said. "I didn't know the slap skates made such a difference in the curves. Maybe I'll get myself a pair."

Speed skaters wear gloves and a lightweight, tight-fitting uniform that is designed to reduce wind resistance. They also wear protective equipment such as helmets, knee pads, and shin guards.

Every event in speed skating (also called long track racing) is held on a 437-yard (400-meter) track. Competitors skate around the track a predetermined number of times, depending on the length of the contest. The walls of the small speed skating rinks are padded to protect the skaters, who take sharp turns at very high speeds. If the ice surface is too cold, the skaters have more difficulty gliding because the ice becomes coarse, which causes friction. In ideal conditions, a thin layer of water coats the ice, making gliding easier. Skaters prefer a cold surface to one that is too warm, since slushy conditions dramatically reduce speed.

Long track racing demands a variety of skills—quick starts in the shorter races, endurance and strength in the longer ones, and perfect form and speed every time. Long track skating is most widely seen in the Olympic Games and in international meets.

Skaters must make swift, clean starts, and use proper form—powerful leg thrusts and long, smooth arm strokes. During the race, skaters lean forward at the waist with their knees bent, head low, and eyes focused on the track. In races up to 1,500 m, athletes use the two-arm swing, alternating arms with each leg stroke. For longer races they switch to the one-arm swing, in which they tuck one arm behind their backs while swinging the other. They may also clutch both arms behind their backs on straightaways. The slightest imperfection in form may result in added time because of the increased air resistance.

In preliminary heats, two skaters race each other. The competitor with the fastest time wins the heat. Pairs and lane assignments are determined by draw. Most athletes prefer being paired with a fast opponent, since that seems to improve both skaters' performances.

Athletes skate counterclockwise on two separate tracks, which are divided by snow or markers. Since the inside lane is shorter than the outside one, the skaters are required to change lanes each lap. If they simultaneously enter the crossover point, located in the backstretch, the skater in the outside lane has the right of way since he or she had to skate farther to match the opponent.

Depending on the distance of the race, skaters start either side-by-side or staggered. The skater in the inside lane wears a white armband, and the skater in the outside lane wears a red one. Each skater is allowed one false start (leaving before the sound of the gun). A second false start results in disqualification. In such a case, the remaining athlete skates the heat alone.

Racers start by running on their skates until they hit stride, and then continue in smooth, graceful strides. They use the turns to create momentum that propels them down the straightaways in a slingshot motion. Skaters may not cross the lane markers when entering a curve. Should any competitor slide into or obstruct the opponent, the result may be a disqualification.

A skater completes the race when his or her skates touch the finish line. An electric beam records time to 1/100th of a second. If two skaters tie after all pairs have skated, they both receive the gold medal. No tiebreakers are run. An athlete who falls during a race may get up and continue, although the chance of making up the lost time is slim, especially in the shorter races.

Men and women compete in five Olympic speed skating events. The men race in the 500-meter, 1,000-meter, 1,500-meter, 5,000-meter, and 10,000-meter events. Women skate the same distances with

A speed skater prepares to race at the 1994 Winter Olympics.

the exception of the 10,000-meter, which is replaced by the 3,000-meter. In all but the shortest race, pairs use a staggered start and skate around the track from 1¼ laps in the 500-meter event to 25 laps in the 10,000-meter. The times for the events last from just over 1 minute in the 500-meter race to more than 13 grueling minutes in the 10,000-meter.

Countries may enter only those skaters who have met or exceeded qualifying times as determined by the International Skating Union. No country may have more than ten women and ten men on its team, and they may enter no more than four competitors in the three short events and no more than three athletes in the two long races.

In the Olympics

The first Winter Olympics in 1924 featured four men's speed skating events. The 1,000-meter race was added in 1976 in Innsbruck, Austria. Women's events did not appear until 1960, at the games in Squaw Valley, California.

American speed skaters have enjoyed great success at the Olympics. The first gold medal in Olympic speed skating history went to Charles Jewtraw of the United States, who edged out two Norwegian skaters to take the 500-meter event. Jewtraw flailed both arms forward and back as he skated but still defeated Oskar Olsen from Norway by two-tenths of a second. Although their success in speed skating events was spotty in the early years, American teams earned numerous speed skating medals over the last three decades of the 20th century.

Finnish athletes swept the remaining three races in 1924. Clas Thunberg won the 1,500-meter and 5,000-meter races, then a silver in the 10,000-meter, when he finished second behind fellow countryman Julius Skutnabb.

Controversy marred the 1932 Olympic Games in Lake Placid, New York. Instead of pairing two speed skaters as is usually done in long track events, American officials introduced the pack style of racing, in which a group of skaters start simultaneously. European athletes, unaccustomed to the congestion, fared poorly, while American competitors took all four gold medals, including two by IRVING JAFFEE

(5,000-meter and 10,000-meter) and two by John Shea (500-meter and 1,500-meter). World record holder Clas Thunberg, who had earned five Olympic gold medals in the previous two games, boycotted the 1932 Olympics in protest.

Irving Jaffee, a skater from New York City, continued the excellent early showing by American athletes in the speed races. Jaffee first learned to skate on roller skates as he delivered newspapers from house to house. Under the guidance of coach Norval Bapte, Jaffee qualified for the 1928 Olympic Games. He posted the fastest time in the 10,000-meter event, but the event was canceled when warm temperatures melted the ice before all the heats were run. Although competitors on several national teams gathered outside the referee's hotel that night to protest the cancellation and to argue that Jaffee should receive the gold medal, no medals were awarded.

A crestfallen Jaffee vowed to win the gold medal in the next Olympics. He intensified his training by skating daily, then spending two hours hiking or jogging. According to Jaffee, the coach and "the rest of the team claimed I was a show-off because I worked so hard," but he refused to be distracted from his goal. Jaffee was rewarded for his hard work when he won double golds in the 5,000-meter and 10,000-meter at the Lake Placid Games.

In a sad turn of events, Jaffee had to give up his gold medals during the Great Depression. In dire need of money, the champion pawned his medals. "By the time I was ready to redeem them," Jaffee said later, "the pawnbroker was out of business."

Norwegian skater Ivar Ballangrud became the first three-time winner when he won gold medals in the 500-meter, 5,000-meter, and 10,000-meter events at the 1936 games. During his Olympic career, the talented Ballangrud captured seven medals, including four gold, two silver, and one bronze.

Skaters returned to Olympic action in 1948, after a 12-year hiatus caused by World War II (1939–1945). Once again, controversy marred one of the speed skating events. Ake Seyffarth of Sweden, a former world record holder, was the favorite in the 5,000-meter. He was so heavily hounded by photographers that, as he entered his final lap, he was forced to swerve to avoid colliding with a photographer who had jumped onto the ice. It cost Seyffarth time and knocked him down to seventh position. Athletes from Norway and Sweden swept all four gold medals, including one by Seyffarth, who rebounded from his earlier disappointment to win the 10,000-meter event.

With emotions from World War II still running high in 1952, members of the Norwegian Olympic Committee banned any athlete from participating in the games—held in their own city of Oslo—who had collaborated with the Nazi occupying forces during the war. Because of this ruling, Finn Hodt, who had gained a spot on the Norwegian team, had to drop out. After being barred from the 1948 Olympics, teams from Germany and Japan—the aggressor nations in World War II—were once again allowed to participate.

Norwegians had plenty to cheer about, though, as Hjalmar Andersen, a truck driver, repeated Ivar Ballangrud's feat by winning gold medals in the 1,500-meter, 5,000-meter, and 10,000-meter events. American skaters took home a gold and a silver in the 500-meter sprint.

Racers from the former Soviet Union rose to dominance in the 1956 games by taking seven medals overall, including four gold. Norwegian athletes, who had won 12 of the 23 gold medals in previous Winter Games, took home only a disappointing silver and bronze.

The Soviet team introduced a scientific approach to speed skating at the 1956 games by bringing in special equipment designed to measure the speed and quality of the ice surface. From that moment on, technology has played a role in the sport. As one observer said at the time, "Russian sports science has replaced Norwegian tradition." Soviet athletes proved their 1956 accomplishment was no fluke by winning six more medals in 1960.

The 1960 games, held in Squaw Valley, California, were memorable because for the first time, women's speed skating events were included. Female athletes competed for gold medals in the 500-meter, 1,000-meter, 1,500-meter, and 3,000-meter races. Soviet women won six medals, including three gold.

American male skaters started to emerge in 1964. Racing on borrowed skates, Richard McDermott, a young barber from Michigan, surprised everyone by upsetting the previous gold medal winner Yevgeni Grischin of the former Soviet Union in the 500-meter event. It would be the only gold medal for the United States in the 1964 games. In preparation for this event, McDermott had trained each afternoon at home by running and lifting weights. He also visited a hypnotist, who put the athlete in a trance and asked him what he needed to do to win the gold medal. When McDermott described the type of race he hoped to run, the hypnotist told him, "For the next two years, you can skate that race every day, and it will be in your subconscious so deep that when you skate in a big race, anywhere, it will be automatic."

On the women's side, Soviet athlete Lydia Skoblikova, who had won two gold medals in 1960, completed one of the most celebrated feats in Olympic history by sweeping all four events in four straight days. Skoblikova was the first athlete, male or female, to win that many gold medals in a single Olympics.

The 1968 games saw an unusual finish in the women's 500-meter sprint when three American skaters tied for second place behind Soviet competitor Ludmila Titova. Mary Meyers, Jennifer Fish, and 16-year-old Dianne Holum each earned a silver medal.

One of the greatest speed skaters in Olympic history, Ard Schenk of the Netherlands, joined Ivar Ballangrud and Hjalmar Andersen as a triple gold medal winner by capturing the 1,500-meter, 5,000-meter, and 10,000-meter events in 1972 at Sapporo, Japan. Female skaters provided plenty of excitement as well. Dianne Holum topped her performance of four years earlier by winning the gold medal in the 1,500-meter event and a silver medal in the 3,000-meter race. One year after the Olympics, the versatile Holum turned to coaching and spent hours working with a 14-year-old skater, ERIC HEIDEN. Under her wise tutelage, Heiden skated to Olympic glory in 1980.

A mishap almost knocked U.S. skater Anne Henning out of contention in the 500-meter race in Sapporo. As she and Canadian skater Sylvia Burka entered the crossover area, Burka, who suffered from impaired vision in one eye, accidentally swerved in front of the American. Henning was forced to straighten up and allow Burka to pass, a move that cost her valuable time. Calling on every ounce of reserve in the final stages of the race, Henning won by less than a third of a second.

Ironically, this victory may have cost her a chance at a second gold medal. Because Henning had been impeded by Burka, her coach lodged a protest. Olympic officials permitted Henning to skate another race by herself and then select the better time as her Olympic finish. (In the solo race, Henning set an Olympic record.) Henning was scheduled to compete in the 1,000-meter event the following day. Weary from her previous day's performances, Henning came in third behind Monika Pflug of West Germany and Atje Keulen-Deelstra of Holland. "I didn't have it," explained Henning. "I woke up feeling like I'd been hit by a truck." Nonetheless, the American skater still had the talent and stamina to take a bronze medal.

Male speed skaters arrived at Innsbruck, Austria, for the 1976 games with the knowledge that they had one

Speed skaters swing one or both arms to increase the power of their forward stroke.

COUNT YOUR BLESSINGS

At the 1998 Winter Olympics, American skater K. C. Boutiette finished fifth in the 1,500-meter speed skating event. Although he had expected to place higher and was disappointed at the outcome, Boutiette did not consider himself a failure: "I just got off bad. I was trying so hard to get back. I was making mistakes I don't usually make. Five years ago, if you had asked me what I'd be doing today, I would probably have said digging ditches. I'm at the Olympics; there is nothing disappointing about that."

more event in which to race for gold. Officials had added a 1,000-meter race, which was won by American skater Peter Mueller.

Sheila Young became the first American ever to win three medals in the Winter Olympics when she defeated the field in the 500-meter sprint, placed second in the 1,500-meter race, and took third in the 1,000-meter event. Young had sold her racing bicycle to raise money so that her fiancé, James Ochowicz, could be there to see her skate. The move paid off handsomely. Young explained later that the moral support from her future husband spurred her to greater effort: "As I came around the first turn I could hear Jim screaming, 'Fight, fight, fight!'"

The Lake Placid games in 1980 produced one of the most memorable performances in all of Olympic history. Eric Heiden swept all five events to become the first athlete to win five individual gold medals in a single Olympics. The same year was the beginning of a series of successes for Karin Enke of East Germany. Enke won a gold medal (500-meter) in 1980, two gold (1,000-meter and 1,500-meter) and two silver medals in 1984 (500-meter and 3,000-meter), and two silver medals (1,000-meter and 1,500-meter) and one bronze medal (500-meter) in 1988.

U.S. speed skater Bonnie Blair followed her 1988 gold medal performance in the 500-m race by winning two more gold medals in 1992. She successfully defended in the 500-meter and added a gold in the 1,000-meter race. Two years later in Lillehammer, Norway, Blair picked up her fourth and fifth gold medals with victories in the 500-meter and 1,000-meter events.

The 1994 Olympics set the stage for two dramatic moments in men's speed skating history. Johann-Olav Koss continued the Norwegian tradition of excellence by not only winning three races, but also setting world records in each event. He successfully outskated the field in the 10,000-meter endurance race and easily won the 1,500-meter and 5,000-meter races.

In 1994, a sentimental favorite to win the gold medal was Dan Jansen of the United States. Most observers assumed Jansen would one day win a gold medal in the Olympics. His numerous World Cup victories included world record showings, especially in his specialty race—the 500-meter—and he had trained hard for his chance at a gold medal, the only honor in his sport that he had not achieved. He failed to win a medal in 1984, but he entered the Calgary games in 1988 as the favorite in both short events, the 500-meter and 1,000-meter races. Everyone knew how much a gold medal meant to him. In addition, he had dedicated his training and effort to his sister Jane, who suffered from leukemia.

Three hours before his first race, Jansen received news that his sister had died. He tried to pull himself together and focus for the two races, but the shaken skater fell in both and finished far out of contention. Distraught by the loss of Jane—the two were very close—and again failing to win a medal, Jansen left Calgary greatly discouraged.

Jansen continued to excel at international speed skating meets. When he broke the world record in the 500-meter three weeks before the 1992 games in Albertville, France, Jansen appeared ready for a triumphant rebound. But, as luck would have it, Jansen again failed to win a medal.

The 1994 games became his last opportunity for gold. He had been competing for more than a decade, and fresher, younger athletes from Europe and elsewhere were staking their claims on world recognition. The 28-year-old Jansen tried to shrug off distractions and concentrate on capturing that elusive gold medal.

Jansen appeared to be breezing along in the 500-meter event until the final turn, when he momentarily lost his balance and touched his hand to the ice. The slight delay cost him dearly, and Jansen finished a dismal eighth in a race everyone had expected him to win.

The 1,000-meter event remained, but seven other competitors came to the games with better personal times than Jansen. The American skater told himself to forget the past—the sister whose memory he so wished to honor, the failures, the letdowns—and put his mind on the race. "I thought, 'Skate, just skate.' I figured this was going to be my last Olympic race ever, no matter what happened. I wanted to win because I've had so many world records, world championships and World Cup victories. This was the only thing left for me to do. Because of my story, I had the support of so many people. It seems like I had to quit caring too much to skate my best."

Jansen hit the track in a positive frame of mind. In the next-to-last turn, he slipped and nearly touched the ice, but he quickly righted himself and continued on. As he neared the finish, spectators cheered so wildly that Jansen knew he was posting a good time.

Not only did his performance earn a gold medal, but it also set a new world record. Fellow skaters cheered the popular Jansen, and spectators in the stands rose to their feet to applaud the brave athlete. They tossed flowers, an American flag, and a stuffed animal onto the ice, and his wife, Robin, was so excited she had to be taken to the emergency medical technicians for treatment.

As a jubilant Jansen spoke to reporters, someone interrupted him to hand him a telephone. President Bill Clinton was calling to offer congratulations and to tell him how much the country had been pulling for him. The most memorable moment, however, came as Jansen skated a victory lap in the arena. Carrying his daughter, Jane—named after his late sister—in his arms, Jansen circled the ice, relieved to know that he had finally captured gold.

The 1998 Winter Games in Nagano, Japan, produced a huge surprise in the 1,500-meter women's race when Marianne Timmer of the Netherlands bested Germany's Gunda Niemann-Stirnemann and Chris Witty of the United States. Timmer had not been considered one of the favorites since she had never won a 1,500-meter event, but she hoped to finish somewhere between third and sixth. In her victory, though, she broke her personal best by 2.5 seconds and shattered the world record by .29 seconds. When her ecstatic coach rushed onto the ice to give her a hug, the coach slipped and almost tackled the startled Timmer.

"When I first saw my time, I couldn't believe it," said an elated Timmer. "I had to look ten times to really believe it." She was not the only startled skater. Niemann-Stirnemann added to reporters, "Clearly, there was only one possible reaction: 'Wow.' It was a crazy time, an amazing time, a fantastic time. I didn't expect her to win the gold medal."

Norwegian speed skater Aadne Sondral emerged from the shadow of a giant to finally win a gold medal in the

1,500-meter event. Labeled Norway's "next great skater" since his mid-teens and considered the successor to Norwegian legend Johann Olav Koss, Sondral nevertheless piled one disappointment on top of another. He finished second in the 1,500-meter in the 1992 games, then slipped to fourth in 1994 in Lillehammer. Doubters wondered if Sondral would ever live up to his potential.

"I've been a big talent and a big loser. I've been one who always comes in second," admitted Sondral. He changed that pattern in the 1998 games in Nagano, Japan, with a gold medal in the 1,500-meter event. It did not come easily, however. Jan Bos from the Netherlands skated before Sondral, and Bos performed so well that he cried in joy over what he believed would be the winning time. If Sondral were to win, he would have to break the world record. Sondral rose to the challenge by posting a record time of 1:47.87. "I'm extremely happy. I've been dreaming of this medal as long as I can remember," he said. He even received a congratulatory telegram from Koss, who was working at the games as a television commentator.

Sondral tried to keep things in perspective. "When I was younger, I thought when my race was good, I was king. When my race was bad,

A triumphant Dan Jansen holds his infant daughter Jane, named after his sister who died of cancer.

I was big loser." That attitude brought moments of triumph as well as numerous heartaches for the Norwegian star. Fortunately, he was the beneficiary of some excellent advice. "Somebody told me, 'If I am not man enough without the medal, I will never be man enough with it.' I am the same guy I was an hour ago," he told reporters after the race. "The only difference is that I skated some fast laps."

German speed skater Gunda Niemann-Stirnemann completed a performance reminiscent of Dan Jansen's when she won a gold medal in the 3,000-meter event. Expected to take three gold medals in 1994, Niemann-Stirnemann collected a silver and bronze. She had not lost a race in her specialty, the 3,000-meter, in three years, but at Lillehammer she slipped and crashed to the ice.

"It's part of my history and it made me cry a lot," Niemann-Stirnemann later said. She used that experience as an incentive to do better in 1998 at Nagano. She achieved her goal when she set an Olympic record and edged out teammate Claudia Pechstein to take a gold medal.

Tenley Albright
figure skater

Tenley Albright was born on July 18, 1935, in Newton Center, Massachusetts. Her father, a renowned surgeon, gave Tenley her first pair of ice skates when she was nine, then flooded the backyard so she could practice on the homemade rink. Young Albright worked with a determination normally found in older, more advanced athletes.

While performing at the Skating Club of Boston, Albright impressed nine-time United States champion Maribel Vinson Owen, who soon took her on as a pupil. Vinson said, "There's really nothing at all in Tenley's background or environment to explain her preeminence in skating, except perhaps that it's cold around Boston. I thought she had talent, but like other little girls at the rink, at first she had no great interest in practicing basic figures [the mandatory figure eights]."

To guarantee that she had ice time, Albright awoke around four o'clock every morning and skated until it was time to go to school. She explained, "I had to listen to my music over and over while working out my routines. I couldn't do that with other skaters present, all wanting to play their music, or at least getting sick of mine."

A year into her rigorous practice schedule, however, Albright suffered an attack of nonparalytic poliomyelitis (polio). To strengthen her muscles, Albright skated even more than before. Four months after the illness, she won a junior figure skating championship.

In 1951, Albright won her first United States Championship and placed sixth at the World Championships. The following year she skated to a silver medal at the Winter Olympics in Oslo, Norway, then captured her first World Championship in 1953.

Despite an injured and bandaged right leg, Tenley Albright won the gold medal in figure skating at the 1956 games.

"SMILE!"

Like all figure skaters, Tenley Albright had to excel in many areas. The arduous compulsory figures demanded constant practice, and she had to assemble a program that would impress judges. Proper music, choreography, and costumes had to blend to produce a memorable routine.

Albright excelled at each, but the task was not small. One area in which her coach forced Albright to improve was her demeanor. She sometimes skated with a stoic expression, which her coach feared would bother some of the judges. To overcome this, Vinson frequently stood at the side of the rink during practice and shouted to her pupil, "Smile!"

The shouting paid off. In fact, other skaters joked that Albright started smiling just to get her coach off her back.

Albright spent hours practicing her routines, and her skating showed it. She still detested the compulsory figures, but she loved the freestyle skating portion of the competition. She told one magazine writer, "There's such a wonderful feeling of freedom when you free-skate. It's a feeling of gliding like a bird." She added, "I like the creative side of skating, the opportunity to practice new jumps or dance steps, to fit them to music in my own way, and then to perfect the whole thing."

While training in Italy for the 1956 Winter Olympics, Albright caught her skate in a hole in the ice and fell. The blade of her left skate slashed her right leg. Her father flew to Italy from Massachusetts to treat her injury. Many doubted that Albright would be able to execute her twists and land on the injured leg. Though hampered by pain, Albright practiced for the games, which were set to start in a few weeks.

At the Olympics, Albright stood in first place after the compulsory figures. She faced a formidable rival in the free-skating part of the program in Carol Heiss, a teammate who had already caught the attention of the skating world. Heiss put on a memorable performance, but Albright, ignoring her pain, executed a near-flawless program to win the gold. This was the first time an American woman had earned such an honor.

Coach Vinson said after the victory, "Tenley did a courageous job. She's a true champion to forget her injury under pressure and not to make it an excuse." Following her gold medal performance, Albright returned to Massachusetts. More than 50,000 admirers lined the streets of Newton Center to give their hometown champion a warm welcome.

Albright skated professionally for a brief time so she could pay off the debt incurred by her father during her years of training. After gaining recognition as amateurs, many skaters join an ice show, but Albright wanted to move on to other things. She believed that "skating is expression," and a series of repetitive exhibitions in ice shows would drain the imaginative aspect from her skating.

After paying off her father's $50,000 debt, Albright returned to school to study medicine. She graduated from Harvard University; then, like her father, she opened an office near Boston as a surgeon.

Bonnie Blair
speed skater

Bonnie Blair, nicknamed "Bonnie the Blur," is an American speed skater who became the first woman athlete in United States history to win gold medals at three consecutive Olympics. Blair has captured more medals in the Winter Olympics than any other American—five gold medals and one bronze.

Blair seems to have inherited her love of skating. Born on March 18, 1964, in Cornwall, New York, Blair was the youngest of six children. Every member of the family loved to skate, and four of her five siblings became speed skating champions. Blair put on her first pair of skates at the age of two, slipping them over her street shoes because her feet were so tiny. Blair later told a magazine reporter that she could not remember learning how to skate—it had always been such a natural part of her life.

In 1966, the Blairs moved to Champaign, Illinois. Bonnie entered her first skating competition at age four. Within three years she was competing in the Illinois state championships. During those years, Blair participated in pack skating, in which all competitors skate in a bunch and vie for the inside position, then race to the finish line.

Former Canadian Olympic silver medalist Cathy Priestner convinced Blair to concentrate on speed skating. Under Priestner's coaching, Blair entered her first speed event at the qualifying meet for the 1980 Olympic trials. Although the 16-year-old qualified for the trials on her first attempt, she did not skate fast enough to earn a spot on that year's team.

She immediately set her sights on making the 1984 Olympic team. Her new coach, Mike Crowe, realized that to gain experience and exposure in speed skating, Blair had to enter as many European events as possible. The Blairs did not have the money to pay her expenses, however. The Champaign Police Department came to her rescue, raising funds to underwrite Blair's expenses by selling T-shirts and bumper stickers.

Blair, who is only 5 feet, 5 inches tall, knew she could not challenge the power

Leaning forward to reduce air resistance, Bonnie Blair competes at the 1992 games.

of her taller rivals. She focused instead on perfecting the difficult technique of speed skating, which requires athletes to lean forward as close to the ice as possible. Through rigorous training, Blair developed a near-perfect form. Though she did not capture a medal in Sarajevo, Yugoslavia, in 1984, she performed above expectations for a first-time entrant by finishing eighth in the 500-meter event.

Blair targeted 1988 as her next goal and stepped up her already vigorous training regimen, which included weight lifting, bicycle racing, and roller skating, to prepare for the 1988 Olympics. The hard work paid off as she was crowned the United States sprint champion in the 500-, 1,000-, and 1,500-meter races from 1985 to 1988. Blair headed into the 1988 Winter Olympics with high hopes. All that stood in her way was Christa Rothenburger of East Germany, who had won a gold medal in the 500-meter event four years earlier.

The rivals put on a spectacle for fans. Rothenburger skated first in the 500-meter and broke the world record with a time of 39.12 seconds. To win her first gold medal, Blair knew she had to break a record set only moments earlier. She did it with a time of 39.10 seconds. Later in the week Blair added a bronze medal in the 1,000-meter race.

Before the 1992 Olympics, Blair experienced a minor slump and slipped to fifth place in the world rankings. Under the guidance of her new coach, Peter Mueller, she came back strong and was favored to take the 500- and 1,000-meter events at Albertville, France. She won both and became the first American woman to receive gold medals in two successive Winter Olympics.

Two years later at Lillehammer, Norway—her final Olympics—Blair accomplished her most memorable feat by capturing gold medals in all three sprint races. She became the first American woman to win five gold medals in either Summer or Winter Olympics, topping four-time gold medalists Pat McCormick (diving), Evelyn Ashford (track), and Janet Evans (swimming). In recognition of her tremendous achievement, *Sports Illustrated* named Blair Sportswoman of the Year for 1994.

With her Olympic career now over, Blair focused on finishing college and coaching. Her love for the sport, combined with her immense talent and supreme dedication, have made Blair one of the most respected champions in Olympic history.

Dick Button
figure skater

Richard Totten "Dick" Button was born on July 18, 1929, in Englewood, New Jersey. His interest in figure skating began at age 12, when his father gave him a pair of skates and arranged for lessons. Despite criticism from his first teacher (who remarked to Button's father that the pudgy youth would never learn to skate), Button was dedicated to becoming a good skater. When his father hired one of the top coaches in the sport, Button quickly developed into one of the country's most promising talents. At age 16, Button was already the reigning United States figure skating champion.

Button introduced his first innovative move, the flying camel, at the 1947 World Championships in Stockholm, Sweden. He took the camel spin (in which the skater spins on one leg and extends the other leg parallel to the ice) and then leaped high into the air. The crowd loved his performance, and the Swedish press declared, "Sweden has never seen such elegant skating."

Button perfected his moves and won an Olympic gold medal at the 1948 games in St. Moritz, Switzerland. This time he included the first double axel in competition. One week after his Olympic triumph, Button won the World Figure Skating Championship. In recognition of his achievements, he received the 1949 James E. Sullivan Award, which is given to the top amateur athlete in the United States. Button was the first figure skater to win this prestigious honor. He successfully defended his Olympic gold medal in 1952, thrilling the crowd with the first triple loop jump (three complete revolutions in the air).

Button won five World Championships and seven U.S. titles before turning to professional skating. He later gained distinction as a television commentator for skating events.

Dick Button sails above the ice during his performance at the 1948 games.

Chun Lee-Kyung
speed skater

Born on January 6, 1976, in Choon-book, South Korea, Chun Lee-Kyung began skating when she was eight years old. A year later, she tried short track speed skating. Chun improved so rapidly that she was selected for South Korea's national team. At age 12 she became the youngest athlete to be named to the squad.

Chun made her first Olympic appearance in 1994 at the Lillehammer games. She won the gold medal in the women's 1,000-meter race, defeating Canada's Nathalie Lambert. Chun added a second gold medal in the women's 3,000-meter relay as part of the winning South Korean team, edging out both the Canadian and United States teams.

Chun topped the world's short track speed skaters in the rankings. In 1996, she set a world record in the 1,000-meter event at Lake Placid. Going into the 1998 games at Nagano, Japan, Chun was determined to improve her performance in the 500-meter sprint, an event that had always given her problems. She experienced difficulties in the shorter event because her small size prevented her from battling for the crucial inside position. This meant that she had to overcome the distance disadvantage.

Chun Lee-Kyung raises the South Korean flag in triumph after winning Olympic gold.

Chun captured the bronze medal in the 500-meter sprint at Nagano, placing behind Canada's Annie Perreault and China's Yang Yang. She called this her proudest moment in racing. She had proved that she could also compete successfully at the top level in the shorter event.

Chun skated to the third gold medal in her Olympic career when she helped the South Korean team repeat its victory in the 3,000-meter relay. A few days later, she was involved in one of the most thrilling races in short track speed skating in the women's 1,000-meter event. Skating stride for stride with China's Yang Yang, Chun gained a slight advantage during the final stretch and crossed the finish line no more than the length of a skate blade ahead of her Chinese rival. Chun collapsed in exhaustion, then threw up her arms in celebration of her achievement. In the two Olympic Games, Chun took home four gold medals, one silver, and one bronze.

Björn Daehlie
Nordic skier

One of the most talented athletes in Winter Olympics history, Björn Daehlie was born in Elverum, Norway, on June 19, 1967. Young Daehlie excelled in a variety of sports and did not begin to focus on cross-country skiing until his teens.

Daehlie took the sport of cross-country skiing seriously. "What distinguished me as a teenager was that I was unusually willing to train, summer or winter. Alone, in the dark, with a headlamp, in the rain, I would do intervals on the steep hills in Maura."

Daehlie skied in his first World Cup race in 1987 and then joined the Norwegian national team in time for the 1988 competition. Although he was a reserve skier and did not race in any events, Daehlie used the World Cup experience to his advantage. He won his first World Cup the following year.

The year 1992 turned out to be a dream for Daehlie. He emerged from obscurity at the Albertville Olympics, where he won gold medals in the 15-kilometer, 50-kilometer, and relay, and a silver in the 30-kilometer event. He ended the amazing year by winning his first World Cup title. Daehlie continued to dominate in cross-country skiing by winning four more Olympic medals in 1994 in Lillehammer, Norway (gold in the 10-kilometer and 15-kilometer, silver in the 30-kilometer and relay), and adding overall World Cup titles for 1995 and 1996.

Daehlie posted similar spectacular results at the Olympics in Nagano, Japan, where he twice came from behind to win a race. His one silver (15-kilometer event) and three gold (10-kilometer, 50-kilometer, and relay) medals in the 1998 games in Nagano brought his career total to 12 Olympic medals, the most of any Winter Olympian.

Immediately after his Nagano success, Daehlie flirted with the idea of retiring. He told the press, "Right now I feel I have finished my ski career. I've no motivation." No matter what the future brings, Daehlie's name will remain on the pages of sports history.

Björn Daehlie races toward the finish line during a cross-country race at the 1998 Winter Olympics in Nagano, Japan.

Mike Eruzione
hockey player

Mike Eruzione was born on October 25, 1954, in Winthrop, Massachusetts. He played on four straight Eastern Collegiate Championship hockey squads during his time at Boston University, the last as captain of the team. After graduating, Eruzione joined the Toledo Goaldiggers of the International Hockey League. His hustle earned him the McKenzie Award, which is given each year to the best American player in the league.

Eruzione was selected for the 1980 U.S. Olympic hockey team and headed to Lake Placid, New York. Although the team was not expected to do well, it advanced to the semifinal match against the powerful Soviet Union squad. The Soviets had won the gold medal in every Olympics since 1960. The teams traded goals until midway through the final period, when Eruzione scored the winning goal. The crowd went wild.

"I remember Mark Harrington worked the puck into the corner to [Mark] Pavelich," Eruzione said after the game. "Pavelich just tipped it into the middle. I got it at the blue line and I think their defenseman was screening the goalie. I don't think he [the goalie] saw it." Eruzione blasted an astounding 20-foot wrist shot that put his team ahead for good. The United States won 4-3. The team went on to defeat Finland in the final match 4-2.

When Eruzione walked up to the podium to accept the gold medal, he summoned the entire team to join him as the national anthem played. "I don't think you can put it into words," he later said. "It was 20 guys pulling for each other, never quitting, 60 minutes of good hockey."

Eruzione's spectacular goal and the unexpected U.S. victory helped popularize hockey in the United States. Keith Tkachuk, who scored 50 goals in the National Hockey League in 1995, has never forgotten the impact of that game. "It was great for hockey in the U.S. More and more Americans are playing a factor in the NHL. Maybe that was the starting point. You've got to thank Mike Eruzione for that big goal."

Eruzione retired from competitive hockey after the Olympics. He worked as a television commentator and as a motivational speaker and is currently on the athletic staff at Boston University.

Mike Eruzione received much praise after scoring the winning goal against the Soviet team with only ten minutes left in the game.

Ekaterina Gordeeva and Sergei Grinkov
figure skaters

When one thought of Sergei, the name Ekaterina automatically came to mind. Paired in sports and in life, Ekaterina Gordeeva and Sergei Grinkov fashioned one of the truly romantic matches in sports. Their feelings for each other were evident in their performances in pairs figure skating, where they won World Championship and Olympic gold medals before turning professional in 1991.

They first skated together in 1982, when Gordeeva was 11 and Grinkov was 15. Coaches from the Soviet Union paired them, and they became good friends. In 1986, Gordeeva and Grinkov, still in their teens, upset the defending champions to win their first World Championship.

At first the two were together only at practice and in competitions. Grinkov dated other women, but that changed in 1989 when they fell in love. Gordeeva had matured, and the two spent long hours on the road together touring with a troupe of world champion skaters. They were rarely apart— they practiced, performed, ate, and socialized together.

"He always, always took care of me," Gordeeva told *Sports Illustrated* magazine in 1996. The couple was separated only once, when Grinkov flew to New Jersey for shoulder surgery. "This is the only time I met him at the airport, and I brought with me one rose. After this, we never leave each other again," said Gordeeva.

The romance added a fire to their performances that most other couples lacked. The Russian duo moved audiences as they skated to Tchaikovsky's *Romeo and Juliet,* Beethoven's *Moonlight Sonata,* or Verdi's *Requiem.* Their movements on

Ekaterina Gordeeva and Sergei Grinkov perform at the 1988 Winter Olympics in Calgary, Canada.

AFTER THE TRAGEDY

The terrible pain of losing husband Sergei Grinkov has mellowed somewhat for Ekaterina Gordeeva. As part of one of the most romantic, fluid couples on ice, Gordeeva enchanted audiences and impressed judges. Now, she usually skates alone in ice shows and at charity exhibitions.

Before Sergei's death, skating was clearly her top priority. After that came her duties as a mother. But as she told *Sports Illustrated* magazine, "I will try to change this, to live more for Dasha [nickname for her daughter]. I give too much on the ice. I always did."

the ice were so unified that competitors referred to them as if they were one person.

Gordeeva and Grinkov won their first gold medal at the 1988 Winter Games in Calgary, Canada. They turned professional in 1991 and married that same year. Their only child, daughter Daria, was born in 1992. They performed at ice shows around the world while retaining homes in both Russia and the United States.

When the International Olympic Committee announced that professional athletes could reapply for amateur status to participate in the 1994 games in Lillehammer, Norway, the couple decided to compete for a second gold medal. They wondered whether they could regain the enthusiasm and zeal that had propelled them to their first Olympic victory.

Although they had been away from the intense training schedule of amateur skaters, the pair choreographed a stunning program during which Grinkov sank to his knees on the ice before his beautiful wife. Of the many former professionals who reapplied for amateur status and competed in the 1994 Olympics, only Gordeeva and Grinkov took home a gold medal.

Life was beautiful for the young family, but that changed in November 1995. While practicing in Lake Placid, New York, for an appearance in the "Stars on Ice" show, Grinkov suddenly stopped skating. He complained of feeling dizzy, grasped the boards, and then collapsed. An emergency medical team attempted to revive him, but without success. Grinkov was pronounced dead at the local hospital.

Everyone asked how an athlete in such superb condition could die so suddenly. An autopsy revealed that Grinkov had coronary heart disease, which he had inherited from his father. Two arteries to his heart were blocked, causing the sudden heart attack. Routine stress tests might have revealed the dangerous condition, but since Grinkov was so fit, he never even thought about such tests.

Gordeeva eventually returned to ice skating, but mostly as a singles skater. "I cannot even think of someone else's arms around me, touching me," she once said. "Since I was 11, I touched only Sergei's hand. Never anyone else's. This way I can still think of Sergei around me when I'm skating." In 1996, Gordeeva wrote a best-selling book about their life together, called *My Sergei.*

Georg Hackl
luger

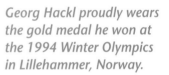

One of the top athletes in luge comes from the German town of Berchtesgaden, deep in the Bavarian Alps. Born on September 9, 1966, Georg Hackl began his career in 1977. He burst onto the world luge scene in 1988 when he won a silver medal in the men's singles event at the Calgary games in Canada.

After honing his skills in world competition and twice winning the World Championships, Hackl returned to the Olympic scene as the heavy favorite in the men's singles. At the Albertville games in 1992, Hackl breezed to victory by posting the three fastest runs in the competition and trouncing his chief rival, Markus Prock.

Two years later Hackl again bested Prock at the Winter Games in Lillehammer, Norway. This time the margin of victory was a slim .013 seconds, the narrowest win ever in an Olympic luge event.

Hackl, called by luge enthusiasts "The Speeding Sausage" because of his swiftness on the course and German heritage, swept all three gold medals in the men's singles when he again topped a strong field at the 1998 Winter Games in Nagano, Japan. His third consecutive medal in the same event placed Hackl in the illustrious company of only five other athletes who had won three straight gold medals: figure skater Gillis Grafström of Sweden; legendary skaters SONJA HENIE of Norway and Irina Rodnina of the former Soviet Union; Ulrich Wehling of the former East Germany, who won the Nordic combined; and United States speed skater BONNIE BLAIR.

Hackl led from start to finish at Nagano. A bit of psychology may have helped him defeat his opponents even before he started down the luge course. Hackl appeared on the first day of competition wearing bright yellow tapered boots. The strange looking boots bothered his rivals, who complained to officials that the boots gave Hackl an unfair aerodynamic advantage. Olympic officials brushed aside the objections, and an amused Hackl sped to Olympic glory by defeating Armin Zoeggeler of Italy by half a second.

Georg Hackl proudly wears the gold medal he won at the 1994 Winter Olympics in Lillehammer, Norway.

Eric Heiden
speed skater

When American sports enthusiasts think of the 1980 Winter Olympics, two events come to mind—the stunning upset of the Soviet Union hockey squad by an unheralded U.S. team, and Eric Arthur Heiden's five gold medals in speed skating. Though Heiden was already a sports hero in Scandinavia, his Olympic feat placed him on the front pages of newspapers across the United States.

Heiden was born in Madison, Wisconsin, on June 14, 1958. As a toddler, he learned how to skate on frozen ponds near his home. Like most Wisconsin boys, he soon found himself with a hockey stick in his hand. When his sister Beth joined a speed skating club, Eric followed along, and his life-long love for the sport began.

Dianne Holum, a former Olympic gold medalist in speed skating, saw Heiden's potential and began coaching him. Holum planned a rigorous training schedule for Heiden. The 14-year-old practiced for hours on the ice, lifted weights, ran, and cycled through the Wisconsin countryside. His hard work paid off.

Heiden placed 7th in the 1,500-meter sprint and 19th in the 5,000-meter race at the 1976 Olympics. He also rose to 5th place at the World Championships. The following year he

Eric Heiden (in front) broke several Olympic records and one world record during his performance at the 1980 games in Lake Placid, New York.

began a string of victories that stunned the speed skating world and made Heiden a hero. In February 1977, he became the first American to win the Men's World Speed Skating Championship, followed by a world junior title and the World Sprint Championship. To Heiden, the triple victories were like a dream.

Heiden repeated his triple victories in 1978 and 1979, setting world records in the process. As the 1980 Olympics at Lake Placid approached, observers picked him as a favorite to take multiple gold medals.

He did not disappoint his fans. On February 15, Heiden won his first gold medal by winning the 500-meter sprint. The next day he set a new Olympic record in the 5,000-meter race and added a second Olympic record by taking the 1,000-meter race on February 19. Two days later, he set yet another Olympic record by capturing the gold medal in the 1,500-meter event in 1:55.44. The only race left was the grueling 10,000-meter. This long race demanded a different set of skills and techniques. Could he defeat a field of athletes who trained solely for the long-distance event?

The night before his final race, Heiden watched from the stands as the underdog United States hockey team defeated the Soviet Union. The upset victory so excited Heiden that he had trouble getting to sleep and overslept. He had little time to prepare for the 10,000-meter. In a display of talent rarely matched, Heiden broke the world record by more than 6 seconds and earned his fifth gold medal of the games.

Olympic marathon runner Bill Rodgers praised his countryman: "What Heiden is doing is comparable to a guy winning everything from the 400 meters to the 10,000 meters in track. My God! Equating it to running, it is doing the impossible!"

Shortly after the Olympics, Heiden retired from speed skating. The quiet young man preferred to remain out of public view. He declined most offers of endorsements and public appearances that typically pour in for Olympic champions. "People ask me to give speeches," he said, "but I'm only 21 years old. What can I tell anybody?" Instead, he focused on a new sport—bicycling. In 1986, he participated in the Tour de France, cycling's most important event. In May 1991, Heiden graduated from Stanford University Medical School in California and began to specialize in orthopedic surgery.

MUSCLES OF THUNDER

Eric Heiden excelled in his sport in part because he worked harder than most of his competitors. He not only won five gold medals, but also set four records—the finest individual performance in Olympic history. One of Heiden's coaches told a newspaper reporter that Eric "is very mind-strong [and] he works hard. If I give the team the afternoon off, most of them will take it. But I always know I will see one lonely figure still working, running down a road to keep his condition. That will be Eric."

His training resulted in stunning victories. A Norwegian coach, Sten Stenson, moaned, "In Norway we say that if you can be good in the 5,000 and 10,000, you cannot do the 500. But Eric can do it. We have no idea how to train to take him. We just hope he retires."

Sonja Henie
figure skater

One of the most extraordinary women to grace the ice, and an athlete who left a lasting impression on her sport, was figure skater Sonja Henie of Norway. Before she finished her amateur career, she had skated to three consecutive Olympic gold medals and ten straight World Championships.

Born on April 8, 1912, in Oslo, Norway, Henie received her first pair of skates at age six. After her first lesson (given by her brother Leif), Henie steadily improved in form and style. The eight-year-old Henie won the Children's Figure Skating Championship in Norway, then the Junior Class C National Contest in the following year.

Guided by her coach, Sweden's Gillis Grafström, a three-time Olympic champion, Henie won the National Figure Skating Championship of Norway in 1923. Even though Henie was only 11, her coach entered her in the 1924 Winter Olympics to give her experience competing at the top level. She placed eighth out of eight spots, but came away with the knowledge and determination that eventually led to an astonishing string of Olympic victories. Henie later wrote that the 1924 Olympics handed her "no honors but a vivid introduction to just how bright the constellation of the world's skating stars was and a heady anticipation of what I might be taking real part in some day."

Henie used her last-place performance as an incentive to do better in 1928. Assisted by her father's wealth, Henie learned from Europe's finest coaches. She trained seven hours each day. She studied ballet, particularly the performances of the influential Russian ballerina Anna Pavlova, so that she could translate her music into movements. She constructed a program based on the "Dying Swan" segment from the ballet *Swan Lake* and perfected 19 different types of spins, one of which she executed a dizzying 80 times before stopping.

"I absorbed so much that it has marked everything I have done since," said Henie. "The ballet was my first love, skating my second. I wanted to bring dancing into skating, to transport the ballet onto ice."

To enhance her routine, Henie became the first skater to wear colorful costumes instead of solid black, and her shorter

HENIE'S OTHER LOVE

Throughout her life, Henie excelled at a wide variety of pursuits. One of those was collecting great works of art. The wealth she had accumulated from her film career and professional skating enabled Henie to buy paintings of the great masters and other artists who would later become famous. With her third husband, shipowner Niels Onstad, Henie acquired original paintings by Pierre-Auguste Renoir, Henri Matisse, Pablo Picasso, and Paul Klee, among others.

skirts provided more freedom of movement as she performed her spectacular spins and jumps.

Henie won her first Olympic gold medal in 1928. Her revolutionary style, which combined the beauty of ballet and the athleticism of figure skating, changed the sport of ice-skating. One reporter watching Henie skate concluded, "Music and her skating are inseparable. With a quick movement, she glides down the ice, gradually gaining speed. Before the onlookers realize it, Sonja is moving in her natural pace, spiraling around the ice on one skate with her arms extended to each side, her head thrown back and a confident smile on her face."

Sonja Henie's combination of grace and athleticism made her one of the greatest figure skaters in Olympic history.

Henie added two more gold medals, one in 1932 at Lake Placid, New York, and another in 1936 at Garmisch-Partenkirchen, Germany. After winning her tenth straight world title later that same year, Henie retired from her amateur career to embark on a new path. She agreed to a series of exhibition appearances in the United States and eventually organized and produced her own ice shows. Because of her reputation, Americans flocked to the performances, and the popularity of figure skating in the United States skyrocketed.

Hollywood capitalized on Henie's immense popularity by casting her in a succession of films. Although none of these movies was a blockbuster in terms of plot or acting, each film included segments in which Henie skated. So many people attended her films that in 1938, Henie ranked third in a Hollywood popularity poll, behind child actor Shirley Temple and heartthrob Clark Gable.

After her film career ended, Henie became a successful businesswomen. In her fabulous nine-year skating career, Henie had won practically every competition she entered. By the time she retired, Henie had accumulated 257 medals and trophies and had changed the style of women's figure skating forever.

Wolfgang Hoppe
bobsledder

The bobsled is one of the most popular Olympic events in Germany. During the 1970s and 1980s, East and West Germany won more Olympic bobsledding medals than any other country, with 10 of the 15 medal spots in the two-man event and 8 of the 15 in the four-man competition.

One of the most talented athletes in this German dynasty—and bobsled history—was Wolfgang Hoppe. Hoppe's big moment came at the 1984 Winter Games in Sarajevo, where he won the gold medal in both the two-man and the four-man bobsled. By doing so, Hoppe became only the fourth driver in Olympic history to take the gold medal in both bobsled events in the same year.

Four years later at Calgary, Hoppe competed again in both events. The Soviet Union team edged him out in the two-man event, and he lost the gold medal in the four-man competition to a team of Swiss athletes. Hoppe earned his fifth Olympic medal in 1992 at Albertville when he drove the German sled to another second-place finish in the four-man event. In Lillehammer, Norway, two years later, a German team again took a gold medal in the four-man event, but it was not Hoppe's team. In a close finish, Hoppe's sled took the bronze medal with a time of 3:28.01, only .23 seconds behind the first-place German team and .17 seconds slower than the runner-up Swiss group.

With gold medals in both the two-man and four-man events, Wolfgang Hoppe (right) became the fourth driver to win two gold medals in the same Olympics.

Hoppe hoped to earn a spot on the German team for the 1998 Olympics in Nagano, Japan, but he failed to qualify. Realizing that his competitive days were behind him, Hoppe retired in May 1998 after compiling the most successful record in bobsled history. The winner of 33 Olympic, World, and European Championships, Hoppe accepted a position training athletes for the German Bobsleigh Federation. The federation president, Klaus Kotter, said, "We want to use Wolfgang's unique experience to make sure we will be as successful in the future as we've been in the past."

Even though he won two gold medals in a sport dominated by Europeans, American speed skater Irving Jaffee is one of the most unheralded athletes to participate in the Winter Olympics. Born on September 15, 1906, in New York City, Jaffee learned to skate on roller skates. For practice, he delivered newspapers each day, roller skating from house to house. At age 14 he took up ice-skating, but his dream was to play on the high school baseball team. When he failed to make the squad, Jaffee switched his focus to speed skating.

Under the guidance of coach Norval Bapte, Jaffee's skating steadily improved. He won his first major event, the Silver Skate race, in 1926. A year later he set a new world record in a 5-mile race. In recognition of his talent, Jaffee was named to the 1928 United States Olympic team.

Jaffee performed well in St. Moritz, Switzerland. Although he missed a bronze medal in the 5,000-meter race by a mere .3 seconds, he recorded the best finish by an American skater. Jaffee was leading all competitors in the 10,000-meter heats when an unexpected rise in the temperature began to melt the ice. Olympic officials postponed the trials, hoping to resume them later. When the temperatures remained warm, they had no choice but to cancel the competition.

Some teammates complained that Jaffee had been denied a medal. Instead of looking back, Jaffee began training for the 1932 Olympics at Lake Placid, New York. He hoped to prove that his performance in the 10,000-meter was no fluke.

Jaffee faced stiff competition in 1932. World record holder Ivar Ballangrud from Norway, who would eventually skate to seven Olympic medals in three games, proved to be Jaffee's toughest rival. Jaffee rose to the challenge. First he won the gold medal in the 5,000-meter race, then defeated Ballangrud by pulling away in the final lap of the 10,000-meter event to beat his rival by five yards.

After Jaffee retired from competitive skating, he toured the United States in a series of skating exhibitions. He died in San Diego, California, on March 20, 1981.

Irving Jaffee poses with his Olympic gold medal at the 1932 games.

Jean-Claude Killy
Alpine skier

In 1968, Jean-Claude Killy skied to gold medals in the slalom, giant slalom, and downhill events.

French Alpine skier Jean-Claude Killy started skiing almost before he could walk. Born on August 30, 1943, in the Paris suburb of Saint-Cloud, Killy was on skis by the time he was three. Since his family spent much time in Val d'Isère, a French resort in the Alps where his father owned a ski lodge, Killy could practice whenever he wanted.

After breaking his leg in competition in 1958 and recovering from a bout with tuberculosis, young Killy won three events in the French junior championships in 1960 and earned a spot on the French national team. His promising career was interrupted two more times between 1962 and 1964, once by a broken ankle and once by service in the French army. He rejoined the French team in time to take part in the 1964 Winter Olympics in Innsbruck, Austria, but his lack of practice became evident during competition, when he fell in the downhill and lost a ski during the slalom.

Between the 1964 and 1968 Olympics, Killy worked on the mental aspect of his sport. After studying his performances and traveling to the United States, where he noticed that skiers seemed to be having more fun, he decided to soften his approach to the sport and adopt a more carefree attitude in his races.

The adjustment seemed to work, because Killy won 12 of 16 meets in the 1966–1967 World Cup season. Killy repeated his World Cup victory the following year and was able to maintain the momentum heading into the 1968 Olympics in Grenoble, France. Performing in front of admiring home fans, Killy scored the "Alpine Skiing Triple" by winning the giant slalom, the slalom, and the downhill. In doing so, he joined Austria's legendary Toni Sailer as one of only two men to sweep the three events in the same Olympics.

Killy had vowed to retire from competitive skiing if he attained the triple victory, and the Frenchman was true to his word: "It is my firm belief that an athlete should retire from sports at the climax of his career. What can I expect more to win than an Olympic gold medal? It's the climax of my career, and that's the end of it."

Johann Olav Koss
speed skater

Johann Olav Koss of Norway put on one of the most memorable performances in Winter Olympic history at the 1994 games in Lillehammer, Norway, by taking three gold medals in men's speed skating. What makes this individual so remarkable is that while he accomplished monumental feats on the ice, off the ice he remained relatively unaffected by his athletic successes.

Born on October 29, 1968, in Oslo, Norway, Koss grew up in a wealthy household. His mother and father worked in the medical field, and they tried to instill in their son a sense of responsibility toward those in need. At the same time, they supported his athletic ambitions, and by 1990, Koss had won the first of his two world speed skating championships.

Koss held the world record in the 10,000-meter race when he arrived in Albertville, France, for the 1992 Winter Games. His smooth rise to success, however, took a temporary turn for the worse. One week before the opening ceremony, Koss was hospitalized with severe stomach pains. Doctors later diagnosed his condition as a blockage in his pancreatic ducts. Although they treated Koss, the incident disrupted his training schedule and his preparation for the games.

Johann Olav Koss raises his arms in triumph after winning Olympic gold at the 1994 games.

He was still so weak that in his first event, the 5,000-meter race, he placed seventh. Two days later, Koss miraculously sped to his first gold medal when he won the 1,500-meter event. He completed a fine Olympics by taking the silver medal in the 10,000-meter competition.

Koss tried to balance the demands of his sport with his dream of becoming a doctor. Between Albertville and the 1994 games at Lillehammer, he pursued his medical studies while maintaining a rigorous training schedule that was designed to put him at his peak as the Olympics approached.

His plan worked. In Lillehammer, Koss entered three races—the 1,500-meter, 5,000-meter, and 10,000-meter—and won three gold medals, setting three new world records. He won the 10,000-meter race by such a huge margin that one opponent claimed the record would stand for 30 years. For his accomplishment, Koss was named *Sports Illustrated* magazine's 1994 Sportsman of the Year—an award he shared with American speed skater BONNIE BLAIR.

Hermann Maier
Alpine skier

Austria's Alpine superhero was born on December 7, 1972, in Flachau, Austria, a village set in the midst of Austrian ski country. While many young Austrians went to the slopes, Maier enjoyed an advantage few others had—his parents owned a ski school. "I began skiing when I was two," he recalled. "It came naturally."

Maier was left off the Austrian national team when he was 15 because the coaches considered him too small and thought he had weak knees. But when he won the European Ski Cup in 1996, he proved that he belonged in the ranks of top skiers, and the Austrian native gained a spot on the squad.

It did not take Maier long to showcase his talent. In his first two years on the World Cup circuit, Maier won ten races, a feat that inspired his teammates to nickname him "Monster" for his performances on the slopes. As the 1998 games in Nagano, Japan, approached, Maier established himself as a clear leader in the five Alpine events (super giant, giant slalom, slalom, combined, and downhill). ALBERTO TOMBA of Italy, who had dominated skiing for the previous ten years, predicted, "It will be difficult to beat Maier in Nagano. He is so full of confidence he can take all the risks he wants."

Hermann Maier sails over a mogul during the downhill event at the 1998 Olympic Games.

Maier's hopes for a gold medal at the games in Nagano faded when he crashed during a downhill run and bruised his left ankle. For a time it looked as if he might miss the remaining events, but Maier recovered sufficiently to win the gold medal in the super-G. A few days after this victory, he defeated teammate Stefan Eberharter in the giant slalom to take his second gold medal.

Maier went on to win the overall title in the 1997–1998 World Cup competition by placing first in every category except the downhill. The following year he captured the overall super-G title and won his second overall World Cup championship in March 2000 at Bormio, Italy.

Andrea Mead Lawrence
Alpine skier

Some athletes have to travel great distances to ski, but Andrea Mead Lawrence merely had to step into her backyard. Born in 1932, Andrea Mead benefited from the fact that her parents, Bradford and Janet Mead, owned and operated the Pico Peak ski resort in Vermont. When the family vacationed, they usually headed to Switzerland to ski in the Swiss Alps. On one of those overseas trips, when Andrea was six, her parents signed a contract with noted instructor Carl Acker to work at their ski school. Mead would enjoy not only the unlimited use of her family's ski slopes, but also the guidance of a respected professional coach.

Five years later, Mead was ready to compete against other top skiers in the United States. In 1944, she placed second in the Women's Eastern Slalom Championship and qualified for the United States Olympic team two years later. Although Mead finished in eighth place in the slalom at the 1948 games in St. Moritz, Switzerland, she gained valuable experience.

Though she wanted to win, she refused to let defeat bother her. "I race for fun," she declared. "It's not worthwhile unless you enjoy it. I'm hardly ever nervous before a race. And I absolutely do not feel bad when I lose. Everybody wants to win. But honestly, I don't. I'd just like to do my best."

After taking a brief break to marry fellow skier Dave Lawrence, Andrea headed to Oslo for the 1952 Olympic Games. Miserable conditions and a lack of snow plagued the games. Norwegian soldiers had to shovel snow from nearby gullies and transport it to the slalom hill. The unusual circumstances bothered some of Mead's opponents, but the American athlete put aside any concerns she might have had and skied to a gold medal in the giant slalom.

Mead turned in a more amazing performance three days later in the regular slalom event. During her first of two scheduled runs, Mead snagged a ski on a flagpole shortly after jumping off. She fell in the snow, but somehow quickly recovered and continued the run. She lost four precious seconds in the mishap, but by the time she reached the finish

SIMPLICITY AND SOUND VALUES

Andrea Mead Lawrence picked up all the values she needed for success from her parents. Bradford and Janet Mead believed in living simply, and they instilled in their children a love of the outdoors and self-reliance.

Janet Mead once explained, "People often speak of Andy's poise. I believe it comes from the simplicity of her childhood. Brad and I had ideas that some people call foolhardy." Janet and Bradford's system of values obviously worked.

Andrea Mead Lawrence receives a victory kiss from her husband following her victory at the 1952 games.

line, she had regained 3 of these seconds and trailed the first-round leader by barely more than one second.

"Mainly, I just want to do well—which is why when I fell I didn't give up," Mead explained. "I didn't want to look bad. I didn't think I would win, but I thought I could. I just threw caution to the wind."

Her husband David, also in Oslo as an Olympian, lent his support. "I've learned never to wish her good luck on race day," he said. "It makes her mad. I just tell her to have fun." Have fun she did, as Mead skied one of her fastest and most daring runs in the second round of the slalom. Tearing down the slopes with almost reckless abandon, Mead posted a time no one could even get close to. "I knew what I had to do," she explained, "so I just cut loose." Spurring her on was the knowledge that her husband, David, stood at the finish line. "David waits at the end of the course for me. When I start, I know he'll be waiting with open arms, so I speed like the devil." Mead's victory made her the first American to win two gold medals in Olympic ski competition.

Four years after her stunning victory, Mead returned to the Olympics. She knew that she was past her prime, but she wanted one last chance at the Olympic experience. Although she finished well down the list in the slalom, she missed a bronze medal in the giant slalom by only one tenth of a second.

Mead and her husband settled on a ranch in Colorado and raised three children. Mead never regretted leaving competitive skiing after the 1956 Olympics: "That's it. No more skiing. My family comes first."

Matti Nykänen
ski jumper

Scandinavians regard Finnish ski jumper Matti Nykänen as the greatest ski jumper in history. While some may debate the claim, no one can deny that in the 1980s, Nykänen dominated the sport like few had before him.

Nykänen was born on July 17, 1963, in Jyväskylä, Finland, a town located 170 miles (27 kilometers) north of Helsinki, the nation's capital. The townspeople loved ski jumping so much that they built several ski jumps in the area and organized training programs to teach the sport to their children. Nykänen quickly rose to the top of his age group and was competing by age 11. Three years later he jumped from the town's 90-meter hill and landed an impressive 289 feet (88 meters) away. To improve his skills, Nykänen worked harder than his peers and made twice as many practice jumps.

The hard work paid off, and in 1987 he won the Finnish national championship in the 90-meter jump. Two years later Nykänen added a World Cup to his accomplishments. His supremacy in ski jumping was confirmed at the 1984 Winter Games in Sarajevo, Yugoslavia, where he became the first ski jumper to win a gold medal in the 90-meter hill and a silver medal in the 70-meter hill.

Nykänen did even better at Calgary in 1988. He was the first to take home two individual gold medals—winning the 70-meter hill by a huge margin. He added a third gold when he helped the Finnish team win the first-ever men's team ski-jumping competition.

While Nykänen was a huge success on the slopes, he faced difficulties in his personal life. More than once the Finnish coaches dropped him from the national team because of his arrogant attitude and his alcoholism. Nykänen's drinking made him difficult to deal with and worsened the strained relations with teammates. After the Calgary games, Nykänen's athletic performance steadily declined, but he began to stabilize his personal life.

Matti Nykänen sails through the air during a ski-jumping competition.

Frank-Peter Roetsch
biathlete

Frank-Peter Roetsch poses for the cameras after winning gold at the 1988 games in Calgary, Canada.

Born in East Germany in 1964, Frank-Peter Roetsch combined a fondness for snow and hills and an accurate aim with firearms that he developed as part of his job as a police officer. His talent gained Roetsch a spot on the national biathlon team in time for the 1984 Olympics in Sarajevo, Yugoslavia. He competed in all three biathlon events (the 10-kilometer, the 20-kilometer, and the 30-kilometer relay). Roetsch placed seventh in the 10-kilometer and helped the East German team to a fourth-place finish in the relay. He also won a silver medal in the 20-kilometer race when he placed behind West German biathlete Peter Angerer.

Roetsch won his first World Championship in 1985 when he outperformed a field of strong competitors to take the 10-kilometer event. Two years later he soared to the top of the rankings by taking both the 10-kilometer and the 20-kilometer individual events at the World Championships, then adding another first-place finish as a member of the victorious relay team.

Roetsch was hailed as one of the greatest biathletes of all time, but his finest accomplishment was still to come. After his victory at the 1987 World Championships, Roetsch traveled to Calgary, Canada, for the 1988 Winter Olympics as the man to beat. The field of competitors was rich with talent, but he was up to the task. In the 20-kilometer individual event, Roetsch hit 17 of 20 targets to post a time of 56:33.3—nearly 30 seconds ahead of silver medal winner Valeri Medvedtsev of the former Soviet Union. He registered an even better score in the 10-kilometer individual event by hitting 9 of 10 targets to again edge out Medvedtsev. In taking both competitions, Roetsch became the first athlete ever to sweep the individual biathlon events.

Roetsch returned to the games in 1992 at Albertville. This time he placed 9th in the 10-kilometer and a dismal 53rd in his specialty, the 20-kilometer race. Though Germany's team took the gold medal in the relay, Roetsch was not selected as one of the four skiers. He was, however, able to contribute his knowledge and experience to his countrymen. Germany has earned gold medals in the relay event in the 1992, 1994, and 1998 Winter Games.

Gian Simmen
snowboarder

The fast-rising sport of snowboarding made its Olympic debut at the 1998 Winter Games in Nagano, Japan. Daniel Franck from Norway and Ross Powers from the United States arrived as heavy favorites in the halfpipe competition, but a young Swiss snowboarder by the name of Gian Simmen startled everyone by walking off with the gold medal. Simmen exemplified what often occurs in the Olympic Games: an unheralded athlete dreams of victory, then under daunting pressure puts on the performance of a lifetime to win the competition.

Born on February 19, 1977, in Arosa, Switzerland, Simmen became involved in winter sports at an early age. The fun-loving athlete took up snowboarding because he thought it looked exciting and offered a different sort of challenge from the typical Alpine and Nordic winter events. Though he did well in the sport, he had never won an event before Nagano.

Simmen surged to the lead in the first of two runs in the men's halfpipe competition, which requires athletes to execute a series of twists and turns in the air as they snowboard through a U-shaped trough. Performing in the rain, Simmen received the highest scores of any athlete for aerial maneuvers, distance of jumps, and technical merit. To secure the gold medal, however, Simmen had to execute a second clean ride. While Franck and Powers were expected to rebound in the second round, neither mounted a serious challenge. Franck performed a spectacular routine of aerial maneuvers, but he fell in the middle of the program, dashing his hopes for top Olympic honors.

Gian Simmen performs an aerial maneuver during the halfpipe competition at the 1998 games.

Though Simmen came in fourth in the second run, his combined total for the two runs placed him atop the field and earned him the gold medal. One reporter who watched the event wrote afterward that

NOT YOUR PARENTS' MUSIC

Spectators who attend figure skating or ice dancing performances are treated to a wide variety of music chosen by the skaters and their coaches. The magical strains of Mozart, Bach, and Beethoven mingle with memorable Broadway tunes.

If the spectators leave the skating arena and head to the slopes where snowboarders compete, they will also watch athletes perform to music. But in this case, the hills are alive with a different sound. Mozart is replaced by Queen, Bach by Blondie, Beethoven by Bob Marley. Rock and hip-hop instead of classical music are the sounds in the air. What else would one expect from a sport in which most of the competitors, like Gian Simmen, participate more for the fun than for anything else?

Simmen "came out of nowhere to win the men's event. Under a heavy downpour, he twisted, flipped and spun down the snow trough—his hat flying off during one midair twist—for a two-run total of 85.2 points."

Simmen was just as surprised by his victory as his rivals. "I can't believe it," he told the press. "I don't know what I've done. I've never been riding like this before. Maybe only in my dreams." He admitted that he didn't think he had a chance to win a gold medal, and came to Nagano simply to have a good time. Daniel Franck, although disappointed in his second-place finish, was happy for Simmen. "It was rad to watch," he said later.

When Simmen returned from Nagano, his hometown of Arosa closed all the schools and held a gigantic party at a local disco. Large banners congratulating the 20-year-old athlete hung from many buildings all day long, and people by the dozens came up to shake his hand.

The exciting competition put on by Simmen, Franck, and the other snowboarders brought tremendous publicity to the new sport. Simmen noted later, "Many people saw the Olympics on TV. So maybe more riders will be motivated to train for the next games."

Simmen's stellar Olympic performance pushed him to the forefront in the world of snowboarding. He told reporter Michael Lucas, "It opened doors I had never seen before, but the most important thing to me—no matter what titles they or I have—is going out with friends and snowboarding. It's my life and love and the best thing that's ever happened to me."

Simmen hopes to compete in future Olympics, but realizes this may have been his only moment of glory. Snowboarding puts tremendous strain on an athlete's knees, and Simmen knows that he may not be physically up to the challenge in the years to come. Even if he were never to perform again, Simmen would have no regrets: "If that happens, I will be there [at the next Olympics] and see all of the youngsters doing it." Simmen did not enter snowboarding for honors and medals only. As he also told Lucas, "I want to have fun in the future and be free in my mind—ride snowboards and skateboards around the world." He added, "Snowboarding is not about the Olympics. Snowboarding is not about politics or fame. It's about fun on the board!"

Ingemar Stenmark
Alpine skier

Ingemar Stenmark has been called one of the greatest down-hill skiers of all time. The three-time World Cup champion in the slalom and giant slalom was born on March 18, 1956, in Josesjö, Sweden, a tiny town near the Arctic Circle. He told *Skiing* magazine that he began skiing at age five because in Sweden, "Skiing was about the only thing of interest, so we wanted to do it all the time." He turned to the sport because "It was a thing I could do alone."

Stenmark's hometown had only one small hill that offered enough slope for a short run on skis. Stenmark would rush home from school, lace on his skis, and practice the slalom on the little hill. Fortunately, the hill had artificial lighting, because in the winter months there was barely more than one hour of daylight.

Stenmark won his first national competition in 1965 at age eight. Five years later he was selected to train with the Swedish national junior team after one of the team's coaches, Hermann Nogler, saw Stenmark ski. Nogler watched Stenmark for a week and then said to himself, "'That boy will be a world champion!' You could see the natural talent, the single-mindedness, the way he was hard on himself."

In the early 1970s, the Swedish Skiing Association sent Stenmark, along with other promising young skiers, to train in the Italian Alps. There, Stenmark learned how to navigate more treacherous slopes. He began perfecting the form that later garnered him numerous victories in the slalom and giant slalom.

Stenmark skied to his first World Cup victory on December 17, 1974. Within months he added three more wins, exhibiting a style of skiing that emphasized quick, controlled movements. By shifting his body weight, Stenmark appeared to slip through the gates with the greatest of ease.

More than anything, Stenmark attributed his victories to his tough mental conditioning: "I am convinced that mental attitude has a lot to do with winning." As he prepared for a race, he psyched himself up by recalling harsh

Ingemar Stenmark is one of only four men to win the slalom and giant slalom events at a single Olympics.

THE JOE DIMAGGIO OF SKIING

Ingemar Stenmark broke records left and right in the slalom and giant slalom, but his greatest achievement, one for which he will always be remembered, is his string of 14 straight giant slalom wins in the 1979–1980 season. He was called the "Alpine equivalent of DiMaggio," a comparison to the immortal Yankee baseball player Joe DiMaggio, who gained fame in 1941 by hitting safely in 56 straight games.

Stenmark would have preferred to have his individual glories ignored. When he retired, he brushed aside his individual accomplishments and claimed he would rather have played "a team sport. Then you don't have to be the best all the time to enjoy it. And the team can be good even if you have a bad day. You can share everything with others, success as well as failure."

comments that others had directed at him, redirecting his anger "at the course—at attacking it and beating it."

Observers predicted an Olympic gold medal for Stenmark in the giant slalom at the 1976 games in Innsbruck, Austria. He skied well, but his uneven performance landed Stenmark in third place behind Heini Hemmi and Ernst Good of Switzerland. Though disappointed, Stenmark at least left the games with a bronze medal.

From 1976 to 1978, Stenmark captured three consecutive World Cup championships and in one stretch won 14 straight slalom competitions. Stenmark was so dominant in the 1978 races that he clinched the World Cup title two months before the season ended, prompting the International Skiing Association to change the scoring procedure to prevent another such occurrence. *Time* magazine described Stenmark as having a "gift for doing the impossible in an unhurried, almost languid, offhandedly elegant manner."

Little could slow this determined athlete. During the 1978–1979 season, he smashed legendary JEAN-CLAUDE KILLY's record of 12 slalom and giant slalom World Cup victories in a single season. Everyone predicted that Stenmark would overtake his opponents in the 1980 games and win gold medals in both the slalom and giant slalom.

Stenmark did just that in Lake Placid, New York, but victory did not come easily. On September 14, 1979, during a practice run in the Italian Alps, Stenmark lost control and bounced downhill for more than 100 yards. Unconscious and suffering a severe concussion, Stenmark shook with convulsions and foamed at the mouth. After a rapid recovery, he returned to the slopes and resumed his training for the Olympics.

Stenmark beat out Andreas Wenzel of Liechtenstein and Austria's Hans Enn to win the giant slalom. He then went on to defeat Phil Mahre of the United States and Jacques Lüthy of Switzerland to add a gold medal in the slalom. Trailing after the first round of the slalom, Stenmark clocked the fastest time in his second run and took top honors.

Though others were impressed with his double gold, the quiet Stenmark remained unflustered. A reserved man by nature, Stenmark observed, "History is not important. The important thing is that I am satisfied with myself." His record shows that he is a true champion.

Picabo Street
Alpine skier

One of the most colorful individuals in Olympic Alpine events is American skier Picabo Street. Raised by her parents, Roland and Dee, to be an independent person willing to accept risks, Street hits the slopes with an abandon that to some observers might seem reckless but to her is simply fun.

Street was born on April 3, 1971, in Triumph, Idaho. As she once told a reporter, "Our parents never told us what to do. They always explained the consequences and let us make our own decisions." From her earliest years Picabo had few fears. Interviewed for *Current Biography Yearbook,* her mother said, "My job was to keep her older brother fed and to keep Picabo alive." To keep the curious youngster from walking too close to the nearby cliffs, Dee had to take Picabo by the hand and show her what lay beyond the edge.

Picabo started skiing at age five and quickly fell in love with the sport. Before she graduated from high school, she had risen in the junior rankings and had been chosen for the United States ski team. Accustomed to her own style of skiing, which in Street's case included very little practice, she advanced on pure talent. But when she made the U.S. team at age 17 in 1989 and faced other top-ranked stars, she proved to be a challenge for coaches. Claiming that she was burned out from skiing for so many years, Street refused to train with her teammates. As a result, the coach dropped her from the team.

Her father advised her to either take skiing seriously and begin training in earnest, or forget about skiing altogether. He suggested that she compile a list of reasons for and against remaining in the sport. When Street did so, she discovered that while she

Picabo Street waves to the crowd after winning gold at the 1998 games in Nagano, Japan.

WHAT'S IN
A NAME?

Picabo Street came by her name because of her parents' penchant for the unusual. Hesitant to influence their children, neither Picabo nor her brother had a legal name for the first two years of their lives. The Streets intended to call their children by nicknames until Picabo and her brother were old enough to choose their own names. But when her parents applied for passports to travel overseas, government officials told them that the children had to have names other than "Baby Boy" and "Baby Girl," which were on their birth certificates. Since Picabo loved to play the game of peekaboo, they decided to name her Picabo, the Indian name of a nearby Idaho town.

missed being a "normal" person her age, she didn't want to look back one day and wonder if she could have made it as a championship skier.

Street decided to train wholeheartedly, lose weight, and prepare for a return to the team. In 1991 and 1992 she won the North American Championship Series competitions, and a year later added a silver medal at the World Alpine Ski Championships. "My father set me straight," she said. "I was wandering astray. I came back knowing what I wanted to do."

She traveled to Lillehammer, Norway, for the 1994 Winter Games with little expectation of doing well. She surprised herself and her coaches by placing second in the women's downhill.

That was a warm-up for what was to follow, as Street burst onto the international skiing circuit. She had a dream year in 1995, winning six of nine downhill races in the World Cup circuit to become the first American woman to ever win the World Cup downhill title. For one of the few times in her life, Street was practically speechless as she received the trophy. Winning the World Cup meant she had been able to maintain a high level of performance over a period of time. After she again became World Cup champion in 1996, she set her sights on the 1998 Olympics and a gold medal.

Misfortune marred her journey to Nagano, Japan. A year before the games, she severely tore the ligaments in her left knee and had to drop off the circuit for six months. On January 31, 1998, only six days before the games were to begin, a binding on her left ski snapped and caused the ski to fly off. Street lost control and crashed head-on into a fence. Although she lost consciousness for a few minutes, Street miraculously walked away from the accident.

Still bearing bruises, Street competed in the super-G on February 11. After almost falling in the opening moments, she raced down the hill to victory. She told reporters afterward that the crash a few days before had actually helped her. "I think I needed a big crash to get my mind off my knee." She added that she was amazed to have done so well. "Everyone comes to the Olympics to win a medal, particularly gold. But to look up there and see my name at the top of the list . . . I just don't know what to say."

Alberto Tomba
Alpine skier

Alberto Tomba was born on December 19, 1966, in the northern Italian town of San Lazzaro di Savena, near Bologna. Tomba's father, who once dreamed of skiing at the top ranks, told his two sons that he expected one of them to become a champion skier. When the father assumed it would be Marco, who at first seemed like a better athlete, Alberto bristled. As he later told *Sports Illustrated,* "My father really didn't believe in me. He thought I would never become a champion. It made me mad. It motivated me."

Tomba worked hard to become a topflight Alpine skier, especially in the slalom and giant slalom events. He abandoned the downhill out of respect for his mother, who feared that her son would injure himself in the faster sport. Marco eventually left skiing for the family business.

By the time he was 18, Tomba had been named to the Italian World Cup team. After two seasons of gaining valuable experience, Tomba embarked on the ten-year run that would make him world famous. He first went on a rigorous diet to lose 15 pounds. At the same time, he perfected a new technique for the events that relied on his sturdy frame (6 feet tall, 200 pounds). Instead of carefully weaving through the gates, Tomba crashed through them, thereby skiing in a straighter

Alberto Tomba's technique of crashing past slalom gates enables him to ski in a straighter line and post a faster time.

WORLD CUP AT LAST

Although Alberto Tomba earned a number of Olympic victories in the 1980s and 1990s, the one trophy that eluded him was the overall World Cup. The winner is determined based on the total points earned by skiers over the course of the year in five areas—slalom, giant slalom, downhill, combined (which includes a slalom and a downhill run), and super giant slalom. Tomba finally achieved this goal in 1994–1995 when he captured the giant slalom and slalom overall titles. He had earned enough points to take the overall World Cup title even though he had competed in only two of the five areas.

line and shaving seconds off his time. His unique style resulted in seven World Cup wins between 1987 and 1988.

By the time he first appeared at the 1988 Olympics in Calgary, Canada, Tomba had earned the respect of the skiing world, even though his attitude often angered coaches. He stuffed ice cubes down teammates' backs, threw spitballs, and thoughtlessly showed up late for team buses and meetings. Some people urged him to change, but as he told *Sports Illustrated,* "I'm considered the clown of my team because I cannot be serious for two minutes. I'm afraid if I become more serious I will stop winning."

Tomba won his first Olympic gold medal in Calgary by cruising to an easy victory in the giant slalom. He then mounted a trademark comeback by storming from third place after the first run to take away the top spot in the slalom from Sweden's INGEMAR STENMARK.

Following the 1988 Olympics, Tomba slackened in his training and mental approach. He loved the attention of his many fans, particularly the women, and spent more time partying than he did practicing. The effects showed up on the slopes as Tomba fell in the rankings. At the 1989 World Championships, Tomba placed seventh in the giant slalom and failed to finish the slalom.

Tomba's father decided to make changes happen. He hired Gustavo Thöni, one of Italy's foremost skiers and a gold medal winner in 1972, as his son's coach. It worked. Tomba regained his form and won six World Cup races in 1990–1991. As he headed into the 1992 Olympic Games in Albertville, France, he was regarded as one of the leading contenders in his events.

Tomba confidently predicted victory. "I will win," he told everyone. "After the games, they will have to change the name of this town to Albertoville," he joked. He backed up his cocky words by winning the gold medal in the giant slalom and a silver medal in the slalom. Tomba became the first skier to successfully defend a gold medal in Alpine skiing. In Lillehammer, Norway, two years later, Tomba added a silver in the slalom to his collection of medals.

Tomba's reign ended in 1998 at Nagano, Japan, where he failed to place in the top three positions in any event. He has since begun to endorse various products and hopes to become a Hollywood actor.

Each sport has its magical moments when an athlete's performance so captures the audience, fellow competitors, and judges that it is talked about for years afterward. The British ice dancing couple of Jayne Torvill and Christopher Dean put on such a show in 1984 at Sarajevo, Yugoslavia.

Born in 1957 in Nottingham, England, Torvill started to train seriously in figure skating at age ten. Within two years, she and partner Michael Hutchinson had won the British Junior Pairs Championship. After Hutchinson left for a new partner, Torvill skated solo for three years before teaming up with Christopher Dean.

Dean, born in Nottingham one year after Torvill, had recently split with his ice dancing partner, with whom he had won the 1971 British Junior Ice Dance Championship. Dean was only able to practice on weekends because he needed the income he earned from his job as a police officer.

Jayne Torvill and Christopher Dean dance across the ice during their performance at the 1994 games.

The team of Torvill and Dean created daring, romantic ice dance routines that brought something new to the sport. Their dramatic performances earned them a string of impressive victories. In 1978, they won their first of seven British championships. This was the first of many perfect 6.0 scores for the twosome. After a disappointing fourth-place finish in the 1980 Olympics, Dean resigned from his police officer's job to devote all of his time to skating. To the delight of both skaters, their hometown of Nottingham raised enough money to support them through the 1984 Winter Games.

With more time to practice, rewards soon followed. In 1981, Torvill and Dean skated to both the European and World Championships—repeating the feat the next two years. At the 1982 European Championships they skated such an emotional, romantic routine to George Gershwin's "Summertime" that "there were strong men standing round me with tears running down their faces," one bystander reported. The British pair took ice dancing to new heights. Often

FIRE AND ICE

The famous "Bolero" program brought Torvill and Dean praise from skating fans around the world. The following day Jane Leavy, a *Washington Post* staff writer who covered the 1984 Olympics in Sarajevo, described Torvill and Dean's performance for her readers: "Jayne Torvill and Christopher Dean, the British couple who have redefined ice dancing, turned ice to fire tonight. They skated to the music of 'Bolero,' that haunting, erotic theme, and told a tale of two lovers who cannot be together; so together throw themselves into a lava pit. When their performance was over and they lay sprawled on the ice, the rink had been transformed into a volcano."

their performances were so vibrant with romance that afterward Torvill, emotionally exhausted, had to remind herself to smile when the audience erupted into applause.

The performance for which Torvill and Dean will always be remembered occurred during the 1984 Winter Games in Sarajevo, Yugoslavia. Skating on Valentine's Day, the couple presented a steamy program to Ravel's "Bolero." After slowly rising from a prone position on the ice, it was clear that the two had mesmerized the audience with their sensual choreography. When Torvill and Dean finally ended their dance, the audience burst into applause as they waited for the judges' scores. The audience hushed as three perfect 6.0's from nine judges appeared on the scoreboard for technical skill, then exploded in a second round of cheering when a string of nine perfect scores was posted for artistry. It marked the first time in Olympic figure skating history that anyone had achieved such perfection. Dean later told reporters, "Tonight was the ultimate of our amateur career. It's what we've been working for I don't know how many years. This is like the pinnacle we've been going towards the whole time, since we put on skates. Tonight we reached the pinnacle."

Immediately after the Olympics, Torvill and Dean won yet another World Championship. They then turned professional, skating first with an international tour in 1984–1985, then on a 60-city United States tour in 1986. They starred with the Ice Capades show for two years and, in 1988, organized their own tour with a group of Russian skaters. In 1993, Torvill and Dean took advantage of a special rule that allowed them to be reinstated as amateurs so they could compete in the 1994 Winter Olympics in Lillehammer, Norway. Although they had not skated in the Olympics in ten years, the couple practiced with one object in mind: another gold medal. They presented a solid program, but the talented couple—the oldest in the field—placed third when some of the judges ruled that they had included illegal moves.

Torvill and Dean's amazing ice dancing career left a lasting imprint on the sport. They skated so beautifully together that the chief dance critic of *The New York Times* compared their performances to ballets.

Vladislav Tretiak
hockey goalie

Vladislav Tretiak may be the greatest goalie in hockey history. Born on April 25, 1952, near Moscow in the former Soviet Union, Tretiak loved sports. When he was ten years old, Tretiak spotted a group of boys playing hockey. He stopped to watch them and ended up joining the team.

The future Hall-of-Famer played goalie because it was the only open position on the team. Within five years he had improved so much that he advanced to the famous Central Army Club.

The young player helped the squad win the 1967 national junior title. Two years later, he starred in the team's World Championship. Because of his outstanding play with the junior team, officials rewarded Tretiak by promoting him to backup goalie in the senior club. Tretiak was thrilled to be with experienced players. He focused intensely on becoming the starting goalie. He worked longer and harder in practices than his teammates, and by the end of that first season his wish came true.

With Tretiak on board, the Central Army Club dominated contests all over the world. They won the national championship in 1970 and consecutive World Championships in 1970 and 1971. The following year they added the Olympic gold medal when Tretiak allowed only 13 goals in five games. The team won three more world titles—in 1973, 1974, and 1975. In the 1976 Olympics, Tretiak improved on his earlier performance by holding opposing teams to a mere 11 goals in five games and helping his team win its second gold medal.

After the demoralizing loss to the Americans in the 1980 Olympics, Tretiak led the Soviet team to another three world championships. He retired following the 1984 Olympics, where he again played goalie for the gold-winning Soviet team. In 1989, he was elected to the Hockey Hall of Fame.

Vladislav Tretiak blocks a shot by the U.S. ice hockey team.

Katarina Witt
figure skater

Katarina Witt smiles during her performance at the 1988 games in Calgary, Canada.

Katarina Witt was born in December 1965 in Karl-Marx-Stadt in the former East Germany. As a child she loved to stop each day on her way home from kindergarten and watch the skaters at a neighborhood rink. After pestering her parents to allow her to skate, Witt stepped on the ice and knew, "This is for me."

East Germany's most successful coach, Jutta Müller, took Witt under her wing when the girl was nine, and the two became inseparable. Witt's intense practice sessions began paying off in 1980, when she finished tenth in the World Championships. Two years later she captured six European titles and established herself as a prime contender for the Olympic gold medal in 1984.

Witt excelled in the free skating portion at the Sarajevo Olympics to edge out Rosalynn Sumners of the United States. Spectators, as well as some of the judges, were captivated by Witt's sensual style of skating. One magazine writer called Witt "the warmest thing to hit the Cold War since vodka," and thousands of letters from fans poured in for the beautiful East German skater.

Witt continued to dominate her sport, winning the European and World Championships in 1984 and 1985. But the next year Witt suffered a rare defeat when American skater Debi Thomas upset her in the 1986 World Championships.

Skating to the music of Bizet's *Carmen,* Witt beat Debi Thomas at the 1988 Olympic Games in Calgary, Canada, to take her second gold medal. A writer for *Newsweek* magazine noted, "She hardly seemed to skate. She flirted. In lieu of daring jumps, the East German beauty seemed content to seek points with her coy shrugs, come-hither expressions, and smiling eyes."

In late 1988, Witt began to skate professionally. She joined United States figure skater Brian Boitano in a series of exhibitions and served as a commentator during the 1992 Winter Olympics in Albertville, France. When a special ruling allowed professionals to reapply for amateur status so they could compete in the Olympics, Witt embarked on a comeback. Though she skated well, she placed seventh at the 1994 Olympic Games in Lillehammer, Norway.

THE WINTER GAMES

Year	City, Nation
1924	Chamonix, France
1928	St. Moritz, Switzerland
1932	Lake Placid, New York, USA
1936	Garmisch-Partenkirchen, Germany
1940	cancelled
1944	cancelled
1948	St. Moritz, Switzerland
1952	Oslo, Norway
1956	Cortina d'Ampezzo, Italy
1960	Squaw Valley, California, USA
1964	Innsbruck, Austria
1968	Grenoble, France
1972	Sapporo, Japan
1976	Innsbruck, Austria
1980	Lake Placid, New York, USA
1984	Sarajevo, Yugoslavia
1988	Calgary, Canada
1992	Albertville, France
1994	Lillehammer, Norway
1998	Nagano, Japan
2002	Salt Lake City, Utah, USA

WINTER HIGHLIGHTS

Chamonix 1924

Countries: 16
Participants: 258 (245 men; 13 women)
Sports: 5 **Events:** 14

Country	Gold	Silver	Bronze	Place
Norway	4	7	6	1st
Finland	4	3	3	2nd
Austria	2	1	—	3rd
United States	1	2	1	4th
Switzerland	1	—	1	5th

St. Moritz 1928

Countries: 25
Participants: 464 (438 men; 26 women)
Sports: 6 **Events:** 14

Country	Gold	Silver	Bronze	Place
Norway	6	4	5	1st
United States	2	2	2	2nd
Sweden	2	2	1	3rd
Finland	2	1	1	4th
France	1	—	—	5th

Lake Placid 1932

Countries: 17
Participants: 252 (231 men; 21 women)
Sports: 5 **Events:** 14

Country	Gold	Silver	Bronze	Place
United States	6	4	2	1st
Norway	3	4	3	2nd
Sweden	1	2	—	3rd
Canada	1	1	5	4th
Finland	1	1	1	5th

Garmisch-Partenkirchen 1936

Countries: 28
Participants: 668 (588 men; 80 women)
Sports: 6 **Events:** 17

Country	Gold	Silver	Bronze	Place
Norway	7	5	3	1st
Germany	3	3	—	2nd
Sweden	2	2	3	3rd
Finland	1	2	3	4th
Switzerland	1	2	—	5th

St. Moritz 1948

Countries: 28
Participants: 669 (529 men; 77 women)
Sports: 7 **Events:** 22

Country	Gold	Silver	Bronze	Place
Norway	4	3	3	1st
Sweden	4	3	3	1st
Switzerland	3	4	3	3rd
United States	3	4	2	4th
France	2	1	2	5th

Oslo 1952

Countries: 30
Participants: 694 (585 men; 109 women)
Sports: 6 **Events:** 22

Country	Gold	Silver	Bronze	Place
Norway	7	3	6	1st
United States	4	6	1	2nd
Finland	3	4	2	3rd
Germany	3	2	2	4th
Austria	2	4	2	5th

Cortina d'Ampezzo 1956

Countries: 32
Participants: 820 (688 men; 132 women)
Sports: 6 **Events:** 24

Country	Gold	Silver	Bronze	Place
USSR	7	3	6	1st
Austria	4	3	4	2nd
Finland	3	3	1	3rd
Switzerland	3	2	1	4th
Sweden	2	4	4	5th

Squaw Valley 1960

Countries: 30
Participants: 665 (522 men; 143 women)
Sports: 6 **Events:** 27

Country	Gold	Silver	Bronze	Place
USSR	7	5	9	1st
Germany (combined team)	4	3	1	2nd
United States	3	4	3	3rd
Norway	3	3	—	4th
Sweden	3	2	2	5th

Innsbruck 1964

Countries: 36
Participants: 1,091 (891 men; 200 women)
Sports: 8 **Events:** 34

Country	Gold	Silver	Bronze	Place
USSR	11	8	6	1st
Austria	4	5	3	2nd
Norway	3	6	6	3rd
Finland	3	4	3	4th
France	3	4	—	5th

Grenoble 1968

Countries: 37
Participants: 1,158 (947 men; 211 women)
Sports: 8 **Events:** 35

Country	Gold	Silver	Bronze	Place
Norway	6	6	2	1st
USSR	5	5	3	2nd
France	4	3	2	3rd
Italy	4	—	—	4th
Austria	3	4	4	5th

Sapporo 1972

Countries: 35
Participants: 1,006 (800 men; 206 women)
Sports: 8 **Events:** 35

Country	Gold	Silver	Bronze	Place
USSR	8	5	3	1st
East Germany	4	3	7	2nd
Switzerland	4	3	3	3rd
Netherlands	4	3	2	4th
United States	3	2	3	5th

Innsbruck 1976

Countries: 37
Participants: 1,123 (892 men; 231 women)
Sports: 8 **Events:** 37

Country	Gold	Silver	Bronze	Place
USSR	13	6	8	1st
East Germany	7	5	7	2nd
United States	3	3	4	3rd
Norway	3	3	1	4th
West Germany	2	5	3	5th

Lake Placid 1980

Countries: 37
Participants: 1,072 (839 men; 233 women)
Sports: 8 **Events:** 38

Country	Gold	Silver	Bronze	Place
USSR	10	6	6	1st
East Germany	9	7	7	2nd
United States	6	4	2	3rd
Austria	3	2	2	4th
Sweden	3	—	1	5th

Sarajevo 1984

Countries: 49
Participants: 1,274 (1,000 men; 274 women)
Sports: 8 **Events:** 39

Country	Gold	Silver	Bronze	Place
East Germany	9	9	6	1st
USSR	6	10	9	2nd
United States	4	4	—	3rd
Finland	4	3	6	4th
Sweden	4	2	2	5th

Calgary 1988

Countries: 57
Participants: 1,423 (1,110 men; 313 women)
Sports: 8 **Events:** 46

Country	Gold	Silver	Bronze	Place
USSR	11	9	9	1st
East Germany	9	10	6	2nd
Switzerland	5	5	5	3rd
Finland	4	1	2	4th
Sweden	4	—	2	5th

Albertville 1992

Countries: 64
Participants: 1,801 (1,313 men; 488 women)
Sports: 10 **Events:** 57

Country	Gold	Silver	Bronze	Place
Germany	10	10	6	1st
Unified Team (former USSR)	9	6	8	2nd
Norway	9	6	5	3rd
Austria	6	7	8	4th
United States	5	4	2	5th

Lillehammer 1994

Countries: 67
Participants: 1,737 (1,217 men; 520 women)
Sports: 10 **Events:** 61

Country	Gold	Silver	Bronze	Place
Russia	11	8	4	1st
Norway	10	11	5	1st
Germany	9	7	8	3rd
Italy	7	5	8	4th
United States	6	5	2	5th

Nagano 1998

Countries: 72
Participants: 2,305 (1,517 men; 788 women)
Sports: 12 **Events:** 68

Country	Gold	Silver	Bronze	Place
Germany	12	9	8	1st
Norway	10	10	5	2nd
Russia	9	6	3	3rd
Austria	3	5	9	4th
Canada	6	5	4	5th

GOLD MEDAL TIMES

Listed below are the gold medal winners in selected events.

* **Olympic Record**
** **World Record**

Speed Skating

MEN
1000 meters

1976	Peter Mueller, USA	1:19.32
1980	Eric Heiden, USA.	1:15.18*
1984	Gaetan Boucher, Canada	1:15.80
1988	Nikolai Gulyaev, USSR	1:13.03*
1992	Olaf Zinke, Germany	1:14.85
1994	Dan Jansen, USA.	1:12.43**
1998	Ids Postma, Netherlands.	1:10.64*

5000 meters

1924	Clas Thunberg, Finland.	8:39.0
1928	Ivar Ballangrud, Norway.	8:50.5
1932	Irving Jaffee, USA	9:40.8
1936	Ivar Ballangrud, Norway.	8:19.6*
1948	Reidar Liaklev, Norway	8:29.4
1952	Hjalmar Andersen, Norway.	8:10.6*
1956	Boris Shilkov, USSR	7:48.7*
1960	Viktor Kosichkin, USSR	7:51.3
1964	Knut Johannesen, Norway	7:38.4*
1968	Fred Anton Maier, Norway	7:22.4**
1972	Ard Schenk, Netherlands	7:23.61
1976	Sten Stensen, Norway	7:24.48
1980	Eric Heiden, USA.	7:02.29*

1984	Sven Tomas Gustafson, Sweden	7:12.28
1988	Tomas Gustafson, Sweden	6:44.63**
1992	Geir Karlstad, Norway	6:59.97
1994	Johann Olav Koss, Norway	6:34.96**
1998	Gianni Romme, Netherlands	6:22.20**

WOMEN
1000 meters

1960	Klara Guseva, USSR	1:34.1
1964	Lydia Skoblikova, USSR	1:33.2*
1968	Carolina Geijssen, Netherlands	1:32.6*
1972	Monika Pflug, West Germany	1:31.40*
1976	Tatiana Averina, USSR	1:28.43*
1980	Natalya Petruseva, USSR	1:24.10*
1984	Karen Enke, East Germany	1:21.61*
1988	Christa Rothenburger, East Germany	1:17.65**
1992	Bonnie Blair, USA	1:21.90
1994	Bonnie Blair, USA	1:18.74
1998	Marianne Timmer, Netherlands	1:16.51*

3000 meters

1960	Lydia Skoblikova, USSR	5:14.3
1964	Lydia Skoblikova, USSR	5:14.9
1968	Johanna Schut, Netherlands	4:56.2*
1972	Christina Baas-Kaiser, Netherlands	4:52.14*
1976	Tatiana Averina, USSR	4:45.19*
1980	Bjorg Eva Jensen, Norway	4:32.13*
1984	Andrea Schöne, East Germany	4:24.79*
1988	Yvonne van Gennip, Netherlands	4:11.94**
1992	Gunda Niemann, Germany	4:19.90

| 1994 | Svetlana Bazhanova, Russia | 4:17.43 |
| 1998 | Gunda Niemann-Stirnemann, Germany. | 4:07.29* |

Bobsled

4-MAN (driver in parentheses)

1924	Switzerland (Eduard Scherrer)	5:45.54
1932	USA (William Fiske)	7:53.68
1936	Switzerland (Pierre Musy)	5:19.85
1948	USA (Francis Tyler)	5:20.10
1952	Germany (Andreas Ostler)	5:07.84
1956	Switzerland (Franz Kapus)	5:10.44
1964	Canada (Victor Emery)	4:14.46
1972	Switzerland (Jean Wicki)	4:43.07
1976	East Germany (Meinhard Nehmer)	3:40.43
1980	East Germany (Meinhard Nehmer)	3:59.92
1984	East Germany (Wolfgang Hoppe)	3:20.22
1988	Switzerland (Ekkehard Fasser)	3:47.51
1992	Austria (Ingo Appelt)	3:53.90
1994	Germany (Harold Czudaj)	3:27.78
1998	Germany (Christoph Langen)	2:39.41

Alpine Skiing

MEN
downhill

1948	Henri Oreiller, France	2:55.0
1952	Zeno Colo, Italy	2:30.8
1956	Anton Sailer, Austria	2:52.2
1960	Jean Vuarnet, France	2:06.0
1964	Egon Zimmermann, Austria	2:18.16

1968	Jean-Claude Killy, France	1:59.85
1972	Bernhard Russi, Switzerland	1:51.43
1976	Franz Klammer, Austria	1:45.73
1980	Leonhard Stock, Austria	1:45.50
1984	Bill Johnson, USA	1:45.59
1988	Pirmin Zurbriggen, Switzerland	1:59.63
1992	Patrick Ortlieb, Austria	1:50.37
1994	Tommy Moe, USA	1:45.75
1998	Jean-Luc Cretier, France	1:50.11

WOMEN
downhill

1948	Hedy Schlunegger, Switzerland	2:28.3
1952	Trude Jochum-Beiser, Austria	1:47.1
1956	Madeleine Berthod, Switzerland	1:40.7
1960	Heidi Biebl, West Germany	1:37.6
1964	Christl Haas, Austria	1:55.39
1968	Olga Pall, Austria	1:40.87
1972	Marie-Theres Nadig, Switzerland	1:36.68
1976	Rosi Mittermaier, West Germany	1:46.16
1980	Annemarie Moser-Pröll, Austria	1:37.52
1984	Michela Figini, Switzerland	1:13.36
1988	Marina Kiehl, West Germany	1:25.86
1992	Kerrin Lee-Gartner, Canada	1:52.55
1994	Katja Seizinger, Germany	1:35.93
1998	Katja Seizinger, Germany	1:28.89

SUGGESTED BOOKS

Anderson, Dave. *The Story of the Olympics.* New York: William Morrow and Company, 1996.

* Ballheimer, David, and Chris Oxlade. *Olympics.* (Eyewitness Series.) New York: Dorling Kindersley, 2000.

* Brimner, Larry Dane. *The Winter Olympics.* Danbury, Conn.: Children's Press, 1997.

Cantor, George, et al., eds. *The Olympic Factbook: A Spectator's Guide to the Winter Games.* Detroit: Visible Ink Press, 1997.

Chronicle of the Olympics. New York: Dorling Kindersley Limited, 1998.

* Italia, Robert. *100 Unforgettable Moments in the Winter Olympics.* Minneapolis: ABDO Publishing Company, 1996.

Johnson, William Oscar. *The Olympics.* New York: Bishop Books, Inc., 1996.

Kristy, Davida. *Coubertin's Olympics: How the Games Began.* Minneapolis: Lerner Publishing Group, 1995.

Leder, Jane. *Grace & Glory: A Century of Women in the Olympics.* Chicago: Triumph Books, 1996.

Levinson, David, and Karen Christensen, eds. *Encyclopedia of World Sport.* Denver: ABC-CLIO, 1996.

Mallon, Bill. *Total Olympics: The Complete Record of Every Event in Every Olympics.* New York: Total Sports Publishing, Inc., 2000.

Wallechinsky, David. *The Complete Book of the Winter Olympics.* New York: Overlook Press, 1998.

Woff, Richard. *The Ancient Greek Olympics.* New York: Oxford University Press, 2000.

* Denotes book for younger readers

INDEX

Page numbers in *italics* indicate photographs.

PHOTO CREDITS